My Journey with Christ

Genesis to Revelation

Bob Francis

Grosvenor House
Publishing Limited

Cover design by Brian Jones

This book is published by
Grosvenor House Publishing Ltd
Link House
140 The Broadway, Tolworth, Surrey, KT6 7HT.
www.grosvenorhousepublishing.co.uk

A CIP record for this book
is available from the British Library

Paperback ISBN 978-1-83615-393-1
eBook ISBN 978-1-83615-394-8

Contents

Part Two

Dedication

This work was entrusted to me in the twilight of my life and has been in the making for the last twenty years. Write a book? No! At least, that is what I thought. God has given me this work while the world is shaking in anticipation of Jesus' return.

The book originates from the talks and sermons I have given throughout my journey with Him. It is profoundly prophetic yet firmly rooted in Scripture.

One-third of the sacred Scriptures are prophetic and span the entirety of the Bible; the breadcrumbs are not always visible. I hope the reader will find it easier to follow, as I have included Scripture in the text rather than needing to search for Bible references.

However, diligent workers for Christ will scrutinise everything they hear, read or even think! Every Christian should consider undertaking the journey from Genesis to Revelation at some point.

May God bless your soul as we take this journey together with Christ.

Bob Francis

Acknowledgements

Family and friends have been vital in my journey, and Christ, through His Holy Spirit (my companion), has served as my primary guide and helper, inspiring and challenging me at every turn.

I also want to recognise two individuals who have joined me on this incredible journey.

Dr. Graham Giles MBE earned his degrees from Cambridge University, Spurgeon's College in South London, the University of Exeter and Bucharest University. He is the founder and chair of Europe to Europe, where he leads innovative reforms in justice, health and education. Additionally, he is a scholar of remarkable depth, making impactful and timely contributions. He is a good friend and a guiding light.

Ben Davies, the Pastor of Anchor Community Church in West End, Southampton, is a reflective and thoughtful leader. He has been my reliable partner in leading a Bible school, consistently demonstrating profound insight and understanding of the Scriptures.

Thank you.

Foreword

Bob Francis has embarked on remarkable journeys, even to the depths of vast oceans. Under tremendous pressure, he has learnt the life disciplines required for service, courage, comradeship and expertise. 'Watching and waiting' was the essence of his seasons at sea, in selfless pursuit of safeguarding others.

During the past two decades, Bob explored hidden depths of even more significant consequence in his voyage as a follower of Jesus. An apprentice and exponent of Scripture, from creation to apocalypse, he faithfully sought, studied and shared truths of urgent inner and infinite significance. Bob invites us to join his most courageous mission in *My Journey with Christ (Genesis to Revelation)*, an intimate and urgent exploration of biblical truths, with surprisingly honest observations and timely teachings.

As I write, we are approaching Passover and Easter 2025. In this significant and unusual year, Jews and followers of Jesus from Eastern and Western confessions celebrate their primary festivals of deliverance on the exact dates. Incidentally, it is also the 80th anniversary of the brutal murders of diarists Anne Frank and Dietrich Bonhoeffer—a Jewish girl and a German pastor whose martyrdom made their words of defiant hope immutable. In his book, Bob also explores this mystery of sacrificial faith that unites Jew and Christian under redeeming blood. He draws from the Old and New Testaments, from the Torah to the Gospels, and from the Garden of Eden to the Garden of Gethsemane. Driven by a passion to understand Jesus, the Lamb slain before the creation of the earth, Bob shares truths less frequently proclaimed from pulpits. He boldly follows paths that others might prefer to avoid, leading to conclusions about Israel, the Church, the Way of the Cross and the end times.

Bob's writings form a prophetic pilgrimage, blending personal and biblical revelations. He selects the route and milestones of the road we follow, remaining faithful to our destination while allowing occasional detours for contemplation. It becomes clear that Bob made deeply personal choices that directed his devotional life and defined his theological perspective. For example, regarding eschatology which concerns death, judgement and the final destiny of the soul and humankind, the author had three options: premillennialism, postmillennialism and amillennialism. Premillennialism holds that a seven-year tribulation will precede a thousand-year period during which Christ will reign on the throne of David. Postmillennialism considers that the millennium is an era, rather than a literal thousand years, during which Christ will reign over the earth, not from an earthly throne, but through the gradual increase of the Gospel and its power to change lives. Amillennialism holds that the Kingdom of God was inaugurated through Christ's resurrection, at which point he gained victory over Satan and reigns over his Church.

Hence, Bob interprets how we should approach our discipleship: the authenticity of Scripture, the authority of the Law and Prophets, the importance of understanding where we stand in history, and the imperative to anticipate Jesus' return. A question will be asked of us when time is almost through.

Have you been chasing dragons, or were dragons chasing you?

Dr Graham Giles MBE

Introduction

Christianity is declining in the West, in stark contrast to other countries, particularly in the East, where it faces suppression. Yet, many are turning to our Lord. In Iran, it is claimed that hundreds of thousands of Christians have secretly joined the Body of Christ at great peril, and churches are growing daily. In contrast, here in the United Kingdom, Christianity is rapidly becoming a 'minority religion.'

During the Reformation, Bible critics planted the seeds that transformed the Church into a lukewarm entity. However, our nineteenth-century missionaries brought God's grace to the United Kingdom, which initiated a significant event in the early twentieth century.

The Bible is filled with prophecies that leaders of our assemblies do not regularly teach. Prophecy aims to give the Church hope and encourages us to look forward to our Lord's return. This account describes the unravelling of a crimson cord from Genesis to Revelation. The creation narrative is not just about how God created the heavens and the earth, but also outlines God's plan for redemption. The pattern of creation, by design, is linked to the first Passover Lamb,

Jesus' crucifixion and resurrection, illustrating how Jesus is the 'First Fruits' and took paradise to Heaven. In short, Genesis chapter 1 is both enlightening and prophetic. We will explore the possibility of a 'hidden' day in the creation narrative.

Prophecy is also linked to the Last Supper, which established a New Covenant and a Betrothal. It foreshadows the reality of the Church's rapture. Framing this within 'culture, context and audience' enhances its prophetic nature.

After the last world war, many people from other nations came to this country to help with the rebuilding, but they were not necessarily welcomed. The first chapters recount my journey to the United Kingdom and how the Lord saved my life when I was three months old, floating in a basin on water. However, migrants who came to Britain were not only essential for rebuilding after the last world war; they also served to remind us of the legacy established by spreading the 'Good News' about Jesus during the Empire's time. Over the past decade, there has been a notable decline in faith. The good shepherds are not as good. The established institutions, often called the Church, are being exposed for what they are.

Then, there is Israel and the deception surrounding its existence. This narrative highlights how prophecy loses significance without Israel's presence. From the line of Ishmael and Esau, we establish the ring of fire surrounding her today. Psalm 83 describes events concerning Israel from the time of King David to the present, and we are witnessing its fulfilment now.

I feel compelled to write this account as a wake-up call to the Church, particularly in the United Kingdom, where we remain lukewarm and in a state reminiscent of the period before the last two world wars.

Within the 'Church', there are two categories of individuals: those who genuinely profess to know Jesus and have experienced true inner conversion, and those whose confessions lack substance. At the conclusion of this account, we will investigate 'how we can discern' which group we belong to.

Jesus mentioned that the wide road results in destruction, whereas the narrow road leads to life. He pointed out that only a few discover the path to life. This book aims to support the Church by promoting prophecy, dispelling deception and inspiring us to look towards our imminent redemption. Let us aim to be counted among the 'wise' instead of the 'foolish' within the Body of Christ.

The consequences of a world without God grow increasingly severe every day.

PART ONE

Chapter One - The Title

As I contemplated different titles for this work, none felt quite right. A long time ago, I came across an intriguing phrase in a Bible foreword: 'The Scarlet Thread of Redemption.' I aimed to use that title to represent this book, script or whatever it eventually turns into. However, I settled on the word 'journey' based on feedback from readers who described their experience as a journey while reading this work.

The account summarises discussions shared over the past twenty years that have supported the operation of Bible schools and offered guidance on the Word of the Lord. Thus, the title reflects everything accomplished in this work for Christ.

However, although the theme follows the scarlet thread from Genesis to Revelation, we will diverge from the main path to discuss critical issues. Thus, we will take detours, branching off to savour some delights.

Some of these diversions require time to describe events that, while necessary, do not align with the timeline for unfolding the prophetic narrative defined by the creation story at the beginning of the Bible. The account in Genesis 1 is not solely about creation—it also serves as a redemption framework. We may even encounter some handbrake turns!

For example, 'What did Jesus write in the Dust?' is an episode leading up to Jesus' death that illustrates Christ's righteousness. However, it does not necessarily contribute to the prophetic journey. It must be included to show that Jesus perfectly aligns with God's will.

Discussing the Bible's inerrancy is essential, as some people dismiss its authenticity or allegorise it to fit their beliefs. Additionally, Israel remains a mystery for many; without the Jewish people, the prophecies in the Bible lose their significance. We will refer to various versions of the Bible but will primarily use the New International Version (*NIV, 2011*)[1] throughout this work. Some may raise their eyebrows, but this version is widely recognised and easier to read. There are arguments for different versions, and we will mention them for clarity. We occasionally refer to the New King James Version (*NKJV, 1982*)[2] for comparison.

For years, I was perplexed about which version to trust when studying God's Word. My companion suggested that the Bible is like an onion. It has many layers, and no single version is sufficient. Text can sometimes fail to convey the whole meaning of the author's intent. Have you ever sent a text message and had the recipient misunderstand? That has happened to me several times and can occasionally lead to conflict, sadness or confusion. Having reflected on this, I now own several digital versions of the Bible.

The NIV is a modern translation that is not strictly literal, meaning it is not a 'word-for-word' translation. It aims to balance words and thoughts. I have many versions of the Bible, and when teaching, I primarily use the NIV, the New King James Version (NKJV), and the Young's Literal Translation (YLT)[3], among several others. When we reach Heaven, we will communicate mind-to-mind, thought-to-thought, so there will be no doubt about meaning.

It is worth noting that some versions have been revised to make them more inclusive. So, always have more than one version. However, who am I that you should even cast me a glance askance? The story begins with my ancestors in India.

Chapter Two – The United Kingdom

Over forty years ago, Jesus became an essential part of my life. This encounter with Him was transformative, blessing me with His Spirit and granting me prophetic insight into His Word, but I am not a prophet. This sparked a deep hunger within me to understand and live by the teachings of the Bible, a journey that has broadened my mind and soul, often leading to pitfalls. My Pastor, Ben Davies, called me an Ephesians four teacher (4:11), which amazed me and prompted much reflection.

Now, back to my journey to the United Kingdom. I arrived in London, England, at about twelve months old in early 1952. We were part of what is now known as the 'Windrush Generation', coming here to work and hopefully seek a better life. However, my journey to the United Kingdom began before I was born (Jeremiah 1:5).

Many people, including myself, were brought to the United Kingdom by the Lord for the country's sake. You might wonder why. The blood of many British men and women had been shed over the centuries as they spread the Gospel message worldwide during the era of the British Empire, particularly in the nineteenth century. I mention the missionaries because some other methods were not always righteous. Nevertheless, Christ became known.

The British are now relying on God's grace from this shed blood, and we are running out of that grace. Prophetically, the world is in the end times. God is calling people from those evangelised nations back to the United Kingdom as an extension of that grace to remind them of Christ.

However, revival is in the air. Revival is not merely the spreading of the gospel; it is the awakening of a church that is currently lukewarm. You can only revive something that is nearly dead. This revival is not the kind that is revealed as quickly as past revivals. It is quiet, but God will bring it about with or without us. This account is primarily intended for the Church of Christ in the United Kingdom, but can also be spiritually applied to other countries.

My ancestors came from the Hindi belt of Northern India, although I am not exactly sure of the specific location. Records from that time were scarce, and slavery was undergoing a rebranding. The British called them indentured workers[4], whose job prospects in India were unfavourable. Many emigrated for a better life; my ancestors went to the Caribbean. The first recorded ship to arrive in Jamaica was the 'Blundell Hunter' in 1850; this is the only record of my ancestors' arrival in Jamaica.

In India, promises were made that work would be available abroad and complimentary transportation back home would be provided after one year. Yeah, right! That happened only for a select few and likely at their own expense. For many reasons, my great-great-grandfathers chose to stay and build a life. Their home became Jamaica in the Caribbean, where my mother and father were born. An initial one-year contract was eventually extended to five years because it was deemed unworkable for such a short duration.

In the 1850s, the Lord took me from India and placed my ancestors in Jamaica. My father was born in Jamaica, in the West Indies, but became restless as he grew up. In 1951, he travelled to England and settled in London. I was born in Jamaica in May 1951 and shortly after, he left and took a ship to England.

My mother told me we were caught in a terrible hurricane after Dad left—Hurricane Charley in 1951. It was Jamaica's most staggering and devastating hurricane recorded up until that time as 125mph winds hurtled through St Thomas, Kingston, St Andrew, Port Royal and other southern parishes. Most homes constructed of board and zinc were not prepared for this!

We were at this incident in St. Andrews, but reflecting on it, I felt the hand of the Lord upon me. My mother told me that we hid under a table during the hurricane (whatever good that would have been), and she floated me in a basin on the water, holding on as the devastation passed. I was about three months old and we survived.

Dad paid for us to travel to England when I was about a year old—my journey from India to the Caribbean and then to England. However, God was not finished yet. In my late teens, I briefly became interested in religion, which was a natural development. My parents were Hindu and were influenced in the Caribbean by Roman Catholics, a few Jehovah's Witnesses, and a small amount of Obia (African spellcasting)—a mixture of spiritual confusion and blight.

In my formative years, my mother occasionally sent me to Sunday School with the next-door neighbour's son, and I loved it! Not necessarily the Sunday school, but he had a two-seater Lambretta scooter motorcycle. I would sit on the back seat, hanging on for dear life as we hurtled down the road, vibrating like a jackhammer. I say 'hurtling', but from my recollection, he was responsible and probably not going that fast; it was fantastic and Christ was embedded in my soul.

In my late teens, I decided to try religion. It was hard, failing at every turn, and I flippantly decided, 'Wait until you're 30 years old.' At that time, it seemed like a long way off. God must have been amused; Jesus came into my life at thirty and a half years old, and I have not looked back. That was more than forty years ago.

My companion indicated this was when Jesus started His primary ministry—at thirty years old.

Later, I became restless and looked around for something else. Before my double dealings caught up with me, I had decided at twenty to join the Royal Navy (RN). Initially, I signed up for twelve years, but marriage came and the money was helpful, so eventually extended it to twenty-two years.

God took me away from my family on the road to meeting Jesus. I joined the RN in May 1972 and completed a five-year apprenticeship. After finishing my training, I was given a choice of which ship to serve on, or as we call it in the RN, a draft.

A warship named HMS Tartar was heading to the West Indies and I hoped to use this first draft to visit my birthplace. Being on this ship in the Caribbean would provide an opportunity. I had family there, so was naturally curious to see them. The choice of ship aimed to make us feel included, but it was generally determined by necessity.

My boss asked me to volunteer for HM Submarine Service, but I declined the request. Although it was suggested, it was only for a short time! He volunteered me anyway, and I went to HMS Dolphin for submarine training—all part of God's Plan, not mine. HM Submarine Warspite became my first draft and I joined while she was in a refit.

Towards the end of 1981, a man told me about the Lord and I became a Christian at the age of thirty, just before the Falklands War with Argentina began in 1982. After the 'Cessation of Hostilities,' HM Submarine Warspite was assigned to patrol the Falkland Islands and the coast of Argentina. We conducted the most extended submarine patrol ever made public, spending 111 days submerged and covering just over 30,000 miles. Being nuclear-powered, fuel was not an issue. During that time, we never saw daylight. My wife laughed when I returned; my skin was pale, and considering my ethnicity, it also amused me.

This all occurred shortly after becoming a Christian. We were immediately deployed to the Falklands and joined the war effort. It was during the 'Cessation of Hostilities,' but it was still scary. I worried that being the only born-again Christian among the crew of 116 might somehow affect my newfound faith. Some of the crew attended church on Sunday mornings but seemed uncommitted. I might have been wrong, or it may have been just for the wine at the end of the service.

Being on a submarine as a Christian was not easy, and the changes in my character did not sit well with my shipmates. Though I lost several friends, they carefully disguised their disdain for this new version of me. We returned safely and I had a wonderful time praising and worshipping the Lord in my 'rack,' a coffin-like middle bunk with the curtain drawn for privacy. Some may remember the cassette recorder. I pre-recorded gospel music; listened with my headphones and sung to the Lord in my 'rack.'

My shipmates' dislike was revealed about twenty years later at a submarine reunion. While aboard the submarine, I carried a small New Testament and Psalms book in my shirt pocket, reading as often as possible in plain sight and leaving another Bible nearby. This must have irritated them.

One day, the pocketbook was gone! Searching high and low, it was nowhere to be seen! They asked jokingly about it at this reunion without any prompting! Suddenly, it dawned on me—they had hidden it.

When I met the Lord in September 1981, the experience was not a massive conversion with fanfare and miracles. Having given my life to the Lord, I was prayed for several weeks later to receive the Holy Spirit. That evening, went home feeling no different. The next day, I felt weighed down, lethargic and burdened. It was Thursday. Church had been the previous evening for our midweek gathering, during which they prayed for my baptism in the Spirit. For three days, it felt like carrying something heavy while walking through mud or quicksand, and I was also subdued.

Managing to drag myself to church on Sunday, sat on the first chair available and could not go any further.

As the music started, I raised my heavy hands, and suddenly, a tingling sensation travelled down my arms. The sensation lingered; I felt lighter and lighter, unburdened, and began to sing without effort. This greatly puzzled me because it felt as if a weight had been lifted from within. The church elders suggested that this could be the Holy Spirit completing His work. As I became wiser in the Word, it was at that moment that the 'Certificate of Debt' due to sin was lifted and cancelled from my soul; my sin was nailed to the cross (Colossians 1:2).

I could go on, but the Lord has given me a deep-seated thirst for His Word since then. Very soon after meeting Him, it became apparent that my primary gift was teaching His Word. Reading the Bible from cover to cover several times was a delightful goal. The Old Testament was heavy reading, but succeeded in getting through it. Teaching—forget it, or so I thought.

In my early years with Christ, I was introduced to Roger Price, who died in 1987.[5] He influenced me and had the privilege of meeting him. His base church then was Chichester Christian Fellowship, where he served as an elder. His Basic Bible Study (BBS) series shaped my heart. While travelling back and forth from Clyde Submarine Base in Scotland to my home in Strood, Kent, where my family eventually settled, I listened to the BBS Series, which included 100 talks that kept me occupied during the eight-hour drive. I made this journey for the better part of twelve months.

Reading and writing did not come naturally to me; on the submarine, only read what was necessary. The extent of my reading included technical manuals, operational procedures and electronic documentation. I often wonder why the Lord gave me the gift of teaching. For me, there were other more interesting things in life. When the idea of writing a book entered my mind, I thought, 'No!'

After twenty-two years of service in the RN, I left to join Portsmouth University at the age of forty-seven, where I obtained a science-based degree in education and became a teacher for students aged 11–16. Having a family, a mortgage and three young children in full-time education was daunting. However, the Lord had prepared the ground ahead for us, and these skills became invaluable for teaching and preparing sermons on various topics.

Reading the Old Testament is essential. I have heard Christians claim that since Christ, the Old Testament is no longer relevant; they are mistaken. Over the years, I have come to agree with this assertion attributed to St Augustine;

'The New Testament is the Old Testament revealed, and the Old Testament is the New Testament concealed.'

The prophetic books have been like a magnet for me, and I have given talks and read books like Revelation several times. The last time, it took me a whole year to cover Revelation, following nine months spent on the Book of Daniel. This initiative began during the COVID-19 pandemic with weekly online posts. While leading this group, we conducted an extensive study and gained much knowledge. The study was not perfect, as I got some things wrong, but when trying to solve a mystery, we can sometimes go down blind alleys.

Why should you listen to me about Christ? I am not a qualified theologian, priest or vicar, nor have I attended Bible school or college. I am certainly not famous, nor published anything before. However, listen to my story, and you may discover that God's Holy Spirit gives you the same unction I have experienced for over forty years.

My authority comes from the Lord. In my father's loins, He took me out of India, then to Jamaica, and eventually England. He removed me from my family and placed me in the submarine service, where I did not want to go, and arranged for a meeting with a stranger named Colin, who told me about the Lord. Here is hoping the Lord stirs your soul. Look beyond the words of this account.

The Lord has commissioned me to serve the United Kingdom as He wills, to pray for this once-blessed land, to teach where He calls and to give an account of my hope. He entrusted me with this final task in the twilight of my life.

Chapter Three - Shed Blood

This chapter explains my love for the United Kingdom and its unique place in the heart of God. When the Jews were driven out of the land after Jesus' death and the destruction of the temple, they scattered in all directions of the compass. This also facilitated the dissemination of the Gospel message.

We will focus on the group that migrated to what is now known as Europe. The Jews faced a challenging existence and were never entirely accepted anywhere. However, they found temporary refuge with the British for a season, and some emigrated to the United States.

The eventual acceptance of the Jews led God to bless Britain and the US. Consequently, the British Empire became the most expansive empire ever established in human history, while the United States emerged as a powerful nation.

Many have attempted to connect the dots linking the sons of Jacob to the eventual rise of the small group of islands that would become the United Kingdom. After researching this topic, I believe that the blessing given to Joseph's two sons (Genesis 48) explains the rise of two nations to such extraordinary power—first the United Kingdom and then the United States of America.

The British received a double portion of this blessing, while the US received a single portion. However, there is another reason for our abundant blessings: wherever the British travelled, the gospel message closely followed, and Christ was preached to the nations. Many devoted their lives to this duty given by the Lord.

In the nineteenth century, the British people experienced a surge of confidence. Christianity evolved into an intercontinental message, inspiring missionaries to spread the word of Jesus. Dr Peter Hammond, in his book The Greatest Century of Missions, states, 'If we want the 21st century to be the greatest century of Missions and Revival, we must learn from the Christian pioneers whom God used to make the 19th century (1801–1900) the greatest century of Christian advance so far.'[6]

Many lost their lives. These pioneers were crucial in disseminating the message throughout the British Empire, especially in Asia, Africa and China. In Dr. Hammond's book, the missionaries face the greatest of shocks. As they venture beyond Christendom to the 'uttermost parts of the earth,' they are appalled to discover all the horrors of untamed heathenism.[7]

The Dark Ages and the Reformation ultimately rendered Britain spiritually barren, yet we can still find God's grace amid this. Thanks to the missionaries and faithful followers of God, the Welsh Revivals took place in 1904–5. This was a significant event! God was preparing the United Kingdom for the devastation that would strike the world over the next forty years. He ignited a movement within the Church to rise and abandon its lukewarm ways; otherwise, the nation would not endure. The revivals sparked a widespread return to the Lord and were accompanied by numerous visions. God transformed the British into a praying nation, aiding Britain through the subsequent two world wars.

During both world wars, citizens were called to prayer by their leaders on numerous occasions, with twelve of those instances taking place during World War Two.[8] King George the Sixth and Parliament called the nation to prayer. Churches, cathedrals, schools and community centres overflowed with people on their knees in response to these calls. Additionally, because of this, Christian teachings were introduced into schools through legislation.

God is positioning the world for the end of days. As a church in the United Kingdom, we are lukewarm, desiring acceptance from society. We compromise at every hiccup and remain paralysed. The poison in our society is acceptance.

The grace of past times is waning. Faithful men and women dedicated their lives to spreading the message of Christ, supporting Jewish communities worldwide, and even sacrificing their lives for the cause's sake. Pray that God may heal our land!

God has extended this grace and brought people from nations influenced by the British to share the message of Christ with the United Kingdom, reminding them of the legacy established for our Lord.

Chapter Four - The Pivot

My companion gave me this title. Understanding Bible prophecy can be challenging for all of us. God tells us in His Word what will happen, but as with all His plans, these revelations come in His time.

Let me use a familiar analogy to illustrate how Bible prophecy is constructed. Using the 'Hill and Valley' principle, we can describe our journey through the scriptures. When travelling up and down hills or mountains, we often see peaks in the distance before spotting the valleys below. Looking back, we can observe the landscape we have traversed, which helps us understand what may lie ahead. Bible prophecy lights the way ahead. It not only shares valuable insights that reflect on past events and offer glimpses of the future, but also invites us to embrace the mystery of when these events might unfold.

Reflecting on the prophetic narrative, the Old Testament points towards the New Testament, helping us piece together parts of the puzzle. Let us view the Bible as a whole; it is divided into three sections: the Old Testament, the New Testament and the Intertestamental Period.

Divided into three, you ask? The silence of God between the Old and New Testaments holds just as much significance as the rest. This timeframe is often called 'the years of silence.' However, this silence was overwhelmingly significant! No prophetic messages emerged from God during the period spanning Malachi to Matthew. Nevertheless, Israel's religious and social landscape experienced remarkable changes. Some might argue that texts were created during this gap but are not deemed sacred. Neither Jesus nor the Apostles referenced them, although they would have known about their presence.

By examining Daniel, we gain insights into this period. He spoke of four empires, two of which were the Medo-Persian and Greek empires, laying the groundwork for the time between Malachi and Matthew. If you read Daniel 8, you will find his prophecy regarding these two empires.

Israel was under the Persian Empire's control from 539 to 332 BC. The Persians were lenient and allowed the Jews to practice their religion. They were even permitted to rebuild and worship at the temple (Ezra 1:1–4). This period included the last 100 years of the Old Testament and the first 100 years of the Intertestamental Period. This time of relative peace and contentment was merely the calm before the storm.

Then came the war with Alexander the Great, who defeated the Persians on his journey to establish the

Greek Empire. A student of Aristotle, he was well educated in philosophy and politics. He insisted that Greek culture be promoted everywhere. Daniel foresaw the rise of the Greek Empire. When Alexander conquered a people, he recruited them for his purposes and taught them basic Greek so that they could comprehend the orders given to them. A form of Greek known as 'guttural' or Koine (common) Greek was instilled in these individuals, paving the way for the New Testament to be written and understood in a common language throughout the subsequent empires.

As a result, the Hebrew Old Testament was translated into Greek and became known as the Septuagint.[9] God was paving the way, as Malachi alludes to in the last book of the Old Testament, and we will refer to an interesting verse. Setting the context! After rebuking all the high priests for their lack of care for the people, Malachi speaks this from the Lord:

'Behold, I send My messenger, And he will prepare the way before Me. And the Lord, whom you seek, Will suddenly come to His temple, Even the Messenger of the covenant, In whom you delight. Behold, He is coming,' Says the LORD of hosts (Mal. 3:1, NKJV).

A messenger, John the Baptist, would prepare the way for our Lord Jesus. However, much needed to be done. For the gospel message about Jesus to spread, everyone must understand and communicate in a common tongue. Our Lord did the same when the British Empire was established. Wherever the British went, the English language spread, and the gospel followed closely behind.

The duration between the Old and New Testaments served as a preparatory phase for the arrival of our Lord Jesus Christ. John the Baptist proclaimed the coming of the greatest prophet ever, who would also become the Lamb of God. God may have been silent, but He was at work. He had said all He would until the end of the Old Testament. Once the ground had been prepared, He would send 'The Son' to His people; perhaps they would listen to Him! No matter what happens, He will fulfil all His promises.

That is why this chapter's title is 'The Pivot'; it serves as the balancing point of biblical history. The silence was deafening!

Chapter Five - The Authenticity of the Bible

God is not random, nor does He make mistakes. He is Lord of all, which means He knows both the beginning and the end. He knew us before birth and, under certain circumstances, what choices we would make. We encounter choices like those of Adam and Eve in our everyday lives, one of which is to choose God's way.

If you believe that Jesus is Lord, you must reflect on the truth of what He says about Himself in His word and on all that has been written, much of which has come to pass. He left us a record known as the Bible.

If we do not believe every word of the Bible, we face the danger inherent in the statement, 'I never knew you.' The book contains no errors. Higher critics have never succeeded in disproving any part of the Bible, often quarrelling over words and dates. While we have not been able to verify certain historical events, which has led to criticism, archaeology has consistently demonstrated the Bible's reliability. Let me suggest that the Bible is the most excellent, harmonious, accurate and mathematically perfect book ever composed, not merely written. I chose the word composed because it is a song for the ages, not just a narrative. It contains harmonies and patterns yet to be discovered. The pattern begins in the first book, a woven tapestry of gold and silk.

It can indeed be a puzzle. When starting a jigsaw puzzle, we assemble the edge pieces to establish a framework. Locating all the edge pieces saves time and rationalises the process. Next, we fill in the details. The Old Testament serves as the framework for the New Testament, while the New Testament fills in the details. The Bible holds authority and bears God's stamp of approval, as demonstrated by the prophet Isaiah.

It does not require man's approval. It possesses authority and is assembled perfectly. Those of us who know Christ need not look further. Let me share a glimpse of the careful weaving of Scripture. First and foremost, Jesus endorsed the Old Testament.

'He said to them, "This is what I told you while I was still with you: Everything must be fulfilled that is written about me in the Law of Moses, the Prophets and the Psalms"' (Luke 24:44).

Let us explore the Book of Isaiah, its structure and its arrangement. God bless Stephen Langton for dividing the Bible into chapters and Robert Estienne for splitting it into verses.

The so-called higher critics of the Bible have long criticised the Book of Isaiah, claiming it was composed by two individuals living many years apart. They argue that Isaiah could not have provided such detailed prophecies regarding Cyrus before his birth (Isaiah 44:28). Additionally, they highlight a change in style in the last twenty-seven chapters.

Thus, we understand the theory that the author of the first thirty-nine chapters of Isaiah differs from the author of the last twenty-seven chapters, indicating that the latter was written after the prophecies were fulfilled. There is substantial scriptural evidence that Isaiah authored all sixty-six chapters. Christ Himself quoted from both sections of Isaiah and confirmed Isaiah's role as a prophet (John 12:37–41).

In the New Testament, over twenty quotes from the Book of Isaiah are ascribed to him. About half of these quotes are from the first thirty-nine chapters, while the other half are from the last twenty-seven chapters. However, the beauty of Isaiah lies in its reflection of the entire Bible. Isaiah is often referred to as a 'miniature Bible.' Let us compare the overall layout of the Bible to that of Isaiah.

The Bible contains sixty-six books, divided into two sections: thirty-nine in the Old Testament and twenty-seven in the New Testament. The first thirty-nine chapters describe law, judgement and the Messiah, while the last twenty-seven chapters focus on grace, salvation and the Lamb.

Isaiah contains 66 chapters in total. The first thirty-nine chapters emphasise law, judgement, and the Messiah, whereas the last twenty-seven adopt a gentler tone, discussing Grace, Salvation, and the Lamb.

Genesis chapter 1 addresses the 'heavens and the earth,' and we see that Isaiah also starts in chapter one, where God speaks to both the heavens and the earth. Isaiah chapter sixty-six describes a new heaven and a new earth. The sixty-sixth and final book at the end of the Bible reveals a new heaven and earth.

Matthew is the fortieth book in the entire Bible. Isaiah 40:3 parallels Matthew 3:3.

'A voice of one calling: "In the wilderness prepare the way for the LORD; make straight in the desert a highway for our God"' (Isa. 40:3).

'This is he who was spoken of through the prophet Isaiah: "A voice of one calling in the wilderness, 'Prepare the way for the Lord, make straight paths for him.'" (Matt. 3:3).

The fortieth book in the Bible.

However, Jesus Himself often cited the Old Testament while teaching, which lent authority to its teachings. When tempted, He quoted Deuteronomy 6:13, 6:16 and 8:3. In the Sermon on the Mount, He quoted Exodus 20:13–14. During His confrontations with

Jewish leaders, He quoted not only from Deuteronomy but also from Isaiah and Hosea.

Jesus references John the Baptist in Luke 7:27, quoting Malachi 3:1, and later cites Isaiah 56:7 when cleansing the temple in Luke 19:46. I could continue, but that would take us too far off course; I have lingered longer than intended.

The Bible requires no external authority to validate its inerrancy, prophetic accuracy and ability to convey spiritual and physical truths. If you believe in Christ, you must regard His word as accurate. There are no flaws in Christ; Jesus is the Word made flesh. The Gospel of John emphasises that He is the Word of God made flesh and lived among us. His pedigree and that of the Bible are stated in Revelation 1:17.

'When I saw him, I fell at his feet as though dead. Then he placed his right hand on me and said: "Do not be afraid. I am the First and the Last"' (Rev. 1:17).

When John beheld Christ, his strength failed.

'I am the Living One; I was dead, and now look, I am alive forever! And I hold the keys of death and Hades' (Rev. 1:18).

If you believe in Jesus, it is important to embrace the idea that the Bible He left us is His special book, carrying a unique heritage. This means it is free from errors. While there may be parts that we struggle to explain or understand, we can trust that He will provide answers. The Bible is like an unfolding mystery. Unlike secrets, which are hidden to prevent discovery for many reasons, the mysteries of the Bible are meant to be revealed in God's own time. We are encouraged to ask, seek and be patient. If the Bible is flawed or filled with errors, how can the offer of salvation be trusted? Jesus was there from the beginning. In His discourse with Moses, who was chosen to lead Israel out of Egypt, He reveals His identity and what He should be called.

Moses was a great man, but initially, he struggled with low self-esteem.

Let us go to Exodus 3:

'Moses said to God, "Suppose I go to the Israelites and say to them, 'The God of your fathers has sent me to you,' and they ask me, 'What is his name?' Then what shall I tell them?" God said to Moses, "I AM WHO I AM. This is what you are to say to the Israelites: 'I AM has sent me to you'" (Exod. 3:13–14).

A proclamation of self-sufficiency, self-existence and immediate presence. Omniscient, omnipresent and omnipotent, Jesus is also referred to as the great 'I am.' This is documented in the Gospel of John. There are seven metaphorical 'I am' statements located within that gospel:

- 'I am the light of the world' (John 8:12; 9:5)
- 'I am the bread of life' (John 6:35, 41, 48, 51)
- 'I am the door' (John 10:7)
- 'I am the resurrection and the life' (John 11:25)
- 'I am the good shepherd' (John 10:11,14)
- 'I am the way and the truth and the life' (John 14:6)
- 'I am the true vine' (John 15:1,5)

There are two more 'I am' statements of Jesus in the Gospel of John that are of God's name, as applied by Jesus to Himself. The first instance comes as Jesus responds to a complaint by the Pharisees. 'I tell you the truth,' Jesus says, 'before Abraham was born, I am!' (John 8:58).

Abraham *was*, but I *am*. There is no doubt that the Jews understood Jesus' claim to be God incarnate because they wanted to stone Him (verse 59). So, Jesus is God and the great I am. He was there from the beginning in the Old Testament and the New Testament. His Word is inerrant.

Chapter Six - The Light of the World

Let us revisit Jesus' role as the light of the world, encompassing both physical and spiritual light. 'I am the light of the world' (*John 8:12; 9:5*). This 'I am' statement in John's Gospel comes right before He heals a man who was born blind. Jesus claims to be the light and demonstrates it through His words and actions. The blind man now sees, and light enters this man. Let us examine the account of creation in the Book of Genesis. We either believe this literally or question the words of our Lord.

'In the beginning, God created the heavens and the earth' (Gen. 1:1).

The first part of that sentence states, 'In the beginning,' and we see grace in those first three words of the entire book. This grace implies that whatever happens afterwards has a conclusion. Thank God for that! God initiated time, establishing a beginning and an end. All that transpires during this period on Earth is limited and distinct from eternity. God knew what would happen after He created the heavens and the earth, both spiritually and physically, revealing His grace from the beginning. He anticipated that sin would enter His creation, so He set it within the boundaries of time. God gave all life a choice, including the angels. He created us, and without Him, we become damaged. Choose me, and you will have life; you can have nothing without me. The term 'God' used in Genesis 1:1 is plural. It encompasses the 'I Am' plurality.

Then we come to the creation account, which states it took six days. God rested from all His work on the seventh day. Does God need rest? No, but He is setting a precedent. However, there is a hidden day that we will discuss later. Those who cannot accept by faith that God created the heavens and the earth precisely as described in His account in Genesis 1 rely on their human intellect and knowledge-based reasoning and understanding gained from the Tree of the Knowledge of Good and Evil. Jesus gave His authority by quoting from the Old Testament.

When confronted by Jewish rulers trying to trap Him, he quoted Genesis. They asked if divorce was lawful, and he referred them back to the Pentateuch. What did Moses command?

Let us take a detour into the gospel of Mark.

Some Pharisees tested him by asking, 'Is it lawful for a man to divorce his wife?'
'What did Moses command you?' he replied.
They said, 'Moses permitted a man to write a divorce certificate and send her away.'

'It was because your hearts were hard that Moses wrote you this law,' Jesus replied (Mark 10:2–5).

Your hearts are hardened! In ancient times, surrounding nations often dismissed their wives at the slightest whim, and men faced no consequences. Moses declared that such actions required a proper court of elders to examine the situation and provide a legal document to safeguard her rights. But Jesus goes back further to the Book of Genesis and quotes from Genesis 2:24.

"But at the beginning of creation God 'made them male and female'" (Mark 10:6).

That is the authority of Genesis. He would not quote anything that was not authentic.

God has gifted us with intellect and reason; however, when it comes to His Word, we should refrain from judging what we do not understand. The Bible not only records how God created the heavens and the Earth, but it also provides a pathway to redemption. It is an ideal model, the most important blueprint in human history. Those who do not believe that God created the world in six literal days should reconsider. When God provided us with this account, He knew people would struggle to accept it as written. As indicated, it is not only about creation but also serves as an outline for redemption.

God takes pains to say at the end of each day, 'Evening and Morning.' Christians who are frail in faith attempt to reconcile evolution with this account to ease their beliefs and adapt it to their way of thinking. God could have created the heavens and the Earth instantly, but there was a purpose. He is not as random as some might think. Consider!

In Revelation 20, Jesus locks Satan away after defeating him and judging unbelievers. In the next chapter, a new heaven and earth appear, but there is no account of how they are made; there is no need for one. They are perfect. They have no beginning or end because they are not created in time. Everything happens in an instant. The Old Heaven and Earth took time for God to create, as God obeyed His laws. All that He made 'in the beginning' had an end.

Chapter Seven – Creation and Redemption All in One

In Genesis, God tells us that the earth was covered in darkness on the first day. He then said, 'Let there be light.' He separated the light from the dark. Darkness existed, and we are given no reason why!

'Now the earth was formless and empty, darkness was over the surface of the deep, and the Spirit of God was hovering over the waters' (Gen. 1:2).

The word 'darkness' is not pleasant. In other scriptures of the Old Testament, it is consistently associated with foreboding or wickedness. How is this word used in different contexts? A trip to Job 3:1–5.

In the Book of Job, we encounter a man whom Satan afflicts with God's consent. This concept can be challenging to accept, but we will proceed. Job's friends sat beside him in silence, pondering the abrupt disasters that stripped affluent Job of his wealth and health. In this context, the term 'darkness' is used when Job contemplates his birth.

'May the day of my birth perish,
and the night that said, "A boy is conceived!"
That day—may it turn to darkness;
may God above not care about it;
may no light shine on it' (Job 3:3–4).

'Darkness' is the same word used in Genesis 1:4; it is not good.

God said, "Let there be light," and there was light. God saw that the light was good and separated the light from the darkness. God called the light "day," and the darkness he called "night." And there was evening, and there was morning—the first day (Gen. 1:3–5).

Then on day four, He created light for the earth:

And God said, "Let there be lights in the vault of the sky to separate the day from the night, and let them serve as signs to mark sacred times, and days and years, and let them be lights in the vault of the sky to give light on the earth. And it was so (Gen. 1:14–15).

What was this first light given on day one? It did not physically illuminate the Earth. Paul provides us with a clue. He addresses the light of the gospel and the responsibility of every Christian servant to make the gospel message clear. There can be no veil. Nothing should be hidden or mysterious.

'For God, who said, "Let light shine out of darkness," made his light shine in our hearts to give us the light

of the knowledge of God's glory displayed in the face of Christ' (2 Cor. 4:6).

This was a quote from the very first day of creation. Christ brings light to the world and opposes darkness. The light here is spiritual, and Christ allows it to shine in the hearts of those who know Him. He is the foremost in all creation.

'I am the Alpha and the Omega, the First and the Last, the Beginning and the End' (Rev. 22:13).

He was introduced to the world on the first day of creation. Why? God appointed Jesus as the redeemer for all that follows. This establishes the framework for redemption, which comes from the promise made to the patriarch Abraham. This promise extends from the first day of creation to the end of Revelation. Jesus is the foundation of all creation. All things were created through Him and for Him, and all are sustained in Him. He is the beginning and the end of everything in this age and the next.

Chapter Eight - Death

Before discussing this framework of redemption, we must first establish what happened in the Garden of Eden and what death involves. This will clarify the first three words, 'In the Beginning.'

When Adam and Eve were created, the angels must have been amazed by their beauty and fragility. They were undoubtedly enamoured with Eve. Angels do not require food; their life comes from being in the presence of God. Adam and Eve were perfectly formed, yet earthbound and delicate. These new beings needed food to survive. God gave them vulnerable bodies of flesh that required sustenance.

Adam and Eve were created within the boundaries of 'In the beginning,' as described in the Bible's first three words. This signifies not only a beginning but also an end. Thus, even before he fell from grace, Adam had both a beginning and an end. This explains the purpose of the Tree of Life! God planted a garden called Eden, where Adam and Eve were placed. He gave them food to eat but also planted two trees.

'And Jehovah God taketh the man, and caused him to rest in the garden of Eden, to serve it, and to keep it' (Gen. 2:15 YLT).

Using this translation, we observe something intriguing. At the end of the sentence God states, 'to serve and to keep.' To serve means to tend to the garden as a gardener would. The last word is fascinating; 'to keep' in *Strong's Concordance (1890)* can signify to guard or hedge around. Thus, the question arises: what was he meant to guard against? God knew what would happen; Adam needed to remain vigilant and call on God if he felt concerned. Somehow, he failed because the serpent attacked Eve.

Now, a command from God to Adam.

*And Jehovah God Laith a charge on the man, saying, 'Of every tree of the garden eating thou dost eat; and of the tree of knowledge of good and evil, thou dost not eat of it, for in the day of thine eating of it—**dying thou dost die**'* (Gen. 2:16–17 YLT).

Satan had already fallen; we find the word 'crafty' (Gen. 3:1) used as he sought to deceive. God knew! When you want to bait an animal, you leave something in a trap that lures it into the enclosure. If you desire an outcome, you must control the journey. Adam sinned, but at the same time, God proclaimed Jesus as the answer, and His plan was set into motion. Let us consider the judgement given to Satan. Having delivered a verdict to Adam and Eve, He says to Satan,

'And I will put enmity between you and the woman, and between your offspring and hers; he will crush your head, and you will strike his heel' (Gen. 2:17 NIV).

God judges Satan, and now he realises he will be crushed, understanding that this frail human race will ultimately lead to his demise. The women he deceived will bring about his downfall.

Going back to Genesis 2, where God is talking to Adam. In verses 16 and 17 (YLT), it says he was forbidden to eat from 'the tree of the knowledge of good and evil.' Ultimately, God states, 'in the day,' which means that immediately upon eating it, 'dying he will die.' This last part refers to two deaths. God does not simply say he is going to die, but rather, dying, he will die.

The first part concerns physical death while the last part addresses spiritual death, which is defined as separation from God. Most people are familiar with Eve's deception by the fallen angel named Satan and Adam's subsequent fall into evil. She ate from the Tree of Knowledge of Good and Evil. After pronouncing judgement, God expelled them from the garden; however, subsequent verses offer insights into what sustained them in the Garden of Eden. By eating from the Tree of Life, time would not affect their life force.

So the LORD God banished *him from the Garden of Eden to work the ground from which he had been taken. After he drove the man out, he placed cherubim on the east side of the Garden of Eden and a flaming sword flashing back and forth to guard the way to the Tree of Life* (Gen. 3:23–24).

God casts them out of the garden to cultivate the ground they originated from. Why did God refer to the ground from which Adam was taken? No word or phrase in Moses' account is irrelevant. God does not engage in small talk.

The ground from which Adam emerged was initially shrouded in darkness, and the dust from which God crafted Adam likely contained something significant. Just as a potter shapes an object, the ingredients in the mixture determine its qualities, whether perfect or imperfect. God fashioned Adam perfectly; however, his composition may have had inherent flaws.

God protects access to the Tree of Life. He employs cherubim, symbolising angelic beings that block the path to the Tree of Life. The sword, blazing and described as 'turning every way', further emphasises the 'firewall' established by God. Thus, Adam and Eve, or anyone else afterwards, could not approach the Tree of Life.

The Tree of Life was accessible to both Adam and Eve, sustaining them in the garden. They were trapped in time and this extraordinary tree nourished their life force. However, now, in their state of sin, two things occur. God stated that dying, they will die. Without this tree, the life force given to them would ebb away, leading to their bodily death. However, there are two types of death. The second death occurred when they were expelled from the Garden and the presence of God. Adam could no longer enjoy fellowship with God because of sin, and we now understand that without the shedding of innocent blood, no one can approach God. They could not access the Tree of Life in their current state. If they continued in this rebellious manner, it would result in a terrible blight. Separation from God is actual death. The body decays and dies, while the spirit remains sorrowful, isolated and empty. This would be the greatest torment in 'Gehenna or the fires of hell.' The flames will burn and the worms will consume, but being apart from God would be worse.

Separating Adam and Eve from the Tree of Life signified their inevitable bodily death. Adam lived to the age of 930 (Gen. 5:5). Both were cast out from the presence of our Lord, which led to spiritual death and, ultimately, physical death. Nevertheless, fellowship with God can persist through the shedding of blood. Therefore, spiritual death indicates separation from God. We experience bodily death, leaving the spirit isolated!

Chapter Nine – The Importance of Eve

On the fifth and sixth days of creation, God introduced living creatures to the earth, and on the sixth day, God created mankind.

Then God said, 'Let Us make man in ***Our image,*** *according to Our likeness; let them have dominion over the fish of the sea, over the birds of the air, and over the cattle, over all the earth and over every creeping thing that creeps on the earth.' So God created man in His* ***own*** *image; in the image of God He created him; male and female He created them* (Gen. 1:26–27).

In His image according to likeness. Detour! No one can see God (Hebrew: Elohim), even when ascending to Heaven in the future! Let us turn to Colossians, where Paul describes Christ as the head of the Church.

The Son is the image of the invisible God, the firstborn over all creation. For in him all things were created: things in heaven and on earth, visible and invisible, whether thrones or powers or rulers or authorities; all things have been created through him and for him (Col. 1:15–16).

God is invisible! How can we reconcile this with being made in His image? This is believed to refer to God's triune nature. The scripture says, 'Let us make man in *our* image'—Body, Soul, and Spirit. See also 1 Timothy 1:17 and Hebrews 11:27. The purpose of Christ is to reveal God to us. He is entirely the radiance of God and indeed man. God prepared a body in advance for Him to come to Earth and demonstrate the Father to us.

'For in Christ all the fullness of the Deity lives in bodily form' (Col. 2:9).

We cannot see God because He is present everywhere. He is all-knowing, all-seeing, and all-powerful. He exists in eternity and we cannot perceive eternity, as we are not created that way! However, we can come to know Him through Jesus. We are being transformed into the image of Jesus—God's radiance.

Back on course. Adam was created before Eve and placed in the Garden of Eden. God did not want Adam to be alone (Gen. 2:18). He made Eve to complement Adam, as she was like him, could communicate, and provided companionship. Together, they would experience perfect love, akin to that of the Father, Son, and Holy Spirit.

We know that God spent time with Adam and conversed with him. God brought the animals to him to see what he would name them. Through this interaction, Adam learned about the animals, instilling in him a sense of responsibility. By being in the presence of God, he gained knowledge of his Creator. Adam would not have faced the burdens we encounter today; his thinking would have been flawless, and his intellectual capacity would have been as God intended. He would have needed a good memory to recall all the animals and their names.

Adam learned about God's creation. He was granted authority over all the animals. His role was to tend to the Garden of Eden like a gardener and prepared as a Guardian, Protector and Provider. This characteristic trait of humanity can be traced back to our ancestors and reflects God's nature. Eve was the pinnacle of God's mystery. After the fall, God revealed His creative nature through Eve. Taken from Adam's side, she was fully human. Formed from Adam and taken from His side, she held equal importance as Adam in the grand scheme of things, but in my view, even more!

Genesis 3:1–7 recounts the fall of humanity. Satan targets Eve and deceives her. Adam would have been a more formidable target than Eve, so Satan shapes his strategy through her; it is through Eve that his downfall is orchestrated. In his conversation with Eve, he questions what God has said. She looks at the tree, which becomes irresistibly appealing. Adam joins in without being tempted, fully aware of his actions—deliberate rebellion. Adam is with her. As a protector, he did not fulfil his role; instead of confronting the situation and informing God, he chose to please Eve, implying that Adam was knowingly complicit. The serpent, or Satan, did not address Adam in the written account.

Genesis 3:8–24 explains the consequences of this rebellion. However, when God begins questioning Adam, we witness the 'blame game.' Adam instinctively tries to safeguard himself by blaming God. Sin reveals its ugly nature!

And he said, 'Who told you that you were naked? Have you eaten from the tree that I commanded you not to eat from?'
The man said, 'The woman you put here with me—she gave me some fruit from the tree, and I ate it' (Gen. 3:11–12).

The woman you put there with me! This is your fault. If you had not created her, this would not have happened! God turns to Eve and she blames the serpent. God then judges both, as indicated in verses 15–16.

'And I will put enmity between you and the woman, and between your offspring and hers; he will crush your head, and you will strike his heel.'To the woman he said, 'I will make your pains in childbearing very severe; with painful labor you will give birth to children. Your desire will be for your husband, and he will rule over you' (Gen. 3:15–16).

In *verse 15*, God tells Satan that he will be crushed, and it is through the woman he deceived that his downfall would come via childbirth. Eve's womb reflects the creative nature of God. Sin entered through the man Adam, but through one man, salvation will come in Christ. God held Adam responsible, and it is his seed that transmits sin from generation to generation. Eve is a sinner but does not pass sin down to her offspring. This is why Jesus could be born fully human and sinless: his Father was not Adam. Christ is the image of God—Guardian, Protector, Provider, Creator. Reflected in 'Male and Female,' He created them. Eve bore the Saviour. That is how, as male and female, we are the image of God.

Chapter Ten – The First Passover Lamb

Let us return to the main topic. When the light of Christ was introduced into creation on the first day, the scarlet thread of redemption began in Genesis and carries through to Revelation.

'Then Jesus spoke to them again, saying, "I am the light of the world. He who follows Me shall not walk in darkness, but have the light of life"' (John 8:12).

The redemption thread begins to crystallise within the mystery of the First Passover. When Adam fell from grace, blood had to be spilt to cover their nakedness. What they were hiding behind was insufficient. From Adam to Noah, humanity lived according to its conscience, which stemmed from the Tree of the Knowledge of Good and Evil. This is the origin of man's conscience. Through this innate understanding, man knows what actions to take and what to avoid, yet he often follows his heart. The heart is intrinsically wicked, regardless of salvation. As Christians, with our cooperation, the Holy Spirit helps keep it in check. God had not yet given the Law.

After the flood, God chose Abraham to build a nation for Himself through which our saviour would eventually be born. The scarlet thread grows brighter. Through this nation, He would demonstrate His standards and how people should live. If they are followed, they will be blessed; if not, God will discipline them. Most importantly, the Redeemer would come.

Israel was born by God's will. Abraham's son, Isaac, was born to a man who was dried up in his old age and to an old barren woman. Isaac was a child of promise. A nation would be born through Isaac, and the redeemer would come from this promise. This nation, Israel, was meant to be a light to the world, demonstrating God as a guardian, protector and provider, depending on obedience to the covenant of the Law given through Moses, whose standards brought blessings. Israel was meant to be God's role model, revealing His ways to other nations and making His name known.

The Nation of Israel is the only nation created by the will of God; all other nations emerged from the will of man, primarily through violence, war or attrition. Israel was born through a promise. God understood that Israel would never be able to follow His ways as outlined in the Law, so He introduced the sacrificial system, which would allow them to maintain their relationship even though they broke His Laws; this was conditional upon having no other gods before Him. The nation failed because it did not separate itself from others and followed their terrible ways.

As Christians, we must confess our failures to Christ; we cannot hope to live a holy life before the Father. We are likened to sheep, prone to wandering and eager to follow. Although we are already clean, as Christians, we walk in a dirty world. Let Jesus wash your feet and keep you clean. This requires confessing to Him all our sins daily.

God nurtured this nation from the twelve sons of Isaac, who were raised and developed in Egypt. However, they became enslaved and cried out to God for deliverance. Reluctantly, Moses stepped in. He purged Moses in the wilderness. When he left Egypt, Moses was forty years old. After killing an Egyptian, Moses fled to Midian, where he took a wife. He remained in Midian for forty years before returning to Egypt. This period served as preparation for what lay ahead.

God appoints men, but refining them for His purposes often takes time. Before Abraham died, God promised that through him, all the families of the earth would be blessed and that He would grant His people a land flowing with milk and honey.

Israel was led through the desert during a wilderness season, similar to how Moses was guided to Midian for refinement. He was sent to Egypt to free the nation from slavery, just as Christ liberated us from the bondage of sin and death. It took ten plagues for Pharaoh to release God's people, with the tenth plague causing the most damage. This plague reveals the significance of the 'First Passover Lamb.' The crimson chord takes on greater meaning. Let us explore the Passover Lamb in greater detail. God informed Moses in Exodus 11 that all the firstborn in Egypt would perish, and only after this would Pharaoh permit His people to leave. God instructed Moses that all families must bring a sacrifice into their homes on the tenth Day of Nissan (Exodus 12:3).

The month was Nisan (or Nissan), the first month on the Jewish calendar (according to the Torah), which coincides with March–April on the civil calendar. It is called Chodesh ha-Aviv—the month of spring, as it marks the beginning of the spring months.

This time of the year points to new beginnings. So, they were to keep the lamb for four days and sacrifice it on the fourth day.

Then they are to take some of the blood and put it on the sides and tops of the doorframes of the houses where they eat the lambs. That same night they are to eat the meat roasted over the fire, along with bitter herbs and bread made without yeast (Exod. 12:7–8).

The Passover occurs on the evening of the fourteenth day of Nissan in Israel's religious calendar year. In the future, this will correspond to the Feast of Unleavened Bread instituted by God and given to the nation of Israel. After that, this seven-day Feast would remind them of the speed of their departure. However, let us focus on the lamb. I asked the Lord why the lamb was kept for four days; under the Law of Moses, no other sacrifice had such a rule.

Animals had to be offered without defects, and it was generally required to keep them for inspection. This ensured that the animal was fit and healthy for sacrifice. In the first Passover, God stipulated that the animal must be kept for four days. This puzzled me, so I did some research. This is how my companion has guided me on significant issues. A question arose that I had never even considered. Something I have read takes on a different meaning. I meditated on the four days—just the four days.

The ancient Egyptians worshipped many gods, one of whom was Khnum, the ram god. Bringing a lamb into their homes for four days before slaughtering and eating it would not have been well received by the Egyptians, but at that time, they were fearful, primarily due to the plagues they had already endured. For them, the ram god Khnum was the great potter and creator of humans, as well as the chief deity associated with the source of the Nile. According to my research, Hebrew scholars have proposed several reasons why the lamb needed to be brought into the house for four days on this occasion and slaughtered on the fourth day.

First, it was to ensure that the animal had no defects. While this is reasonable, it did not satisfy me.

The next reason was that family members would care for the animal and grow attached to this ball of white fluff, making it a significant sacrifice to kill and eat it. This did not convince me either.

Next, an act of courage—standing up for their beliefs and following God's command despite the potential danger from the Egyptians—distinguished the Jews and made them worthy of redemption.

This took courage, as the Egyptians would have been angered by bringing lambs into their homes due to the ram god Khnum; that was a real possibility. No Jew, except Christ, holds value on their own before God; that did not convince me either.

The Passover Lamb arrived at the Jewish household on the first day. On the fourth day, they sacrificed the animal and used its blood for protection against death. There was a pattern here somewhere!

I continued to ponder, feeling unsatisfied, until my companion reminded me of the creation story. On the first day of creation, light entered the world. This was not the physical light that illuminated the earth; Jesus is the light of the world and the first in all creation. On the fourth day, the Earth received cosmic light. So, what if the light given to the world on day four represents God's mysterious way of indicating that

Jesus was physically coming into the world to put things right?

In the future, Jesus would be welcomed into Jerusalem. He was accepted and praised, and the people invited Him to enter. Four days later, He was crucified. Before this, He condemned the Pharisees and cleansed the temple. Jesus cursed the fig tree because He sought fruit but found none. The Pharisees tried to trick Him, but this lamb was perfect; He had no defect.

As an aside, I visited Israel a while ago and was eager to see the Garden of Gethsemane. Situated at the base of the Mount of Olives in East Jerusalem, Gethsemane is where Jesus was tested and arrested before his crucifixion. The trees in the garden captivated me with their form, particularly at their base, where they appeared to have grown in agony. There is significant knotting at the base of the trees, with twisted growth on the exposed trunks resembling roots. The trunks looked stressed, desperately trying to break free as the trees reached for the light. These knotted and twisted lower trunk sections reminded me of Jesus' agony in the Garden of Gethsemane that fateful night. Jesus suffered in ways beyond our imagination, but my thoughts drifted to the cross. The lamb was sifted. What agony caused Jesus to sweat blood? (Luke 22:43–45)

God sent an angel to give Jesus the strength to endure this trial. Jesus asked John, Peter and James to pray, but they fell asleep. In verse 44, He sweats blood. This lamb must be perfect, examined and refined. Research indicates that sweating blood is a condition known as Hematidrosis. It can be a symptom of various conditions, primarily caused by stress or high blood pressure. Tiny blood vessels in the skin can break open, allowing blood to seep through sweat glands. Jesus was under immense stress as He faced crucifixion. He knew that the sacrificial law required Him to hang on a tree as a curse.

Deuteronomy 21 relates:

If a man has committed a sin deserving of death, and he is put to death, and you hang him on a tree, his body shall not remain overnight on the tree, but you shall surely bury him that day so that you do not defile the land which the LORD your God is giving you as an inheritance; for he who is hanged is accursed of God (Deut. 21:22–23 NKJV).

Jesus never sinned and did not deserve death; yet, he had to bear the burdens of sinners. He understood the kind of treatment that awaited him. Roman soldiers were infamous for how they treated prisoners. They would beat them to the brink of death and were experts at inflicting such punishment. The whips they used were tipped with hooks. Being alone, he felt depressed, grieved and sorrowful as he approached death. He asked God to take the coming suffering from him, but only if it was God's will. However, it was not just the anticipation of the torment or the terrible hours on the cross that made Jesus so sorrowful. Matthew 27:46 states that the anticipation of carrying the weight of sin caused Jesus to cry out in the garden, even though he had not sinned.

I often think of Him crying out on the cross, '*My God, My God, why have you forsaken me*?' (Matthew 27:46)

For those with family, it is a tremendous blessing. A family provides us security, companionship and a deep sense of belonging, among many other things. I often reflect on my family and would never want to be apart. I have heard that Jesus' cry to God on the cross shows His humanity, but I believe there is even more to this anguished cry. It was not just the humiliation and suffering awaiting Him that caused Him to sweat blood in the garden, nor was it merely the painful experience of being deserted by His disciples or the lies and hatred from His own people that made Him cry out in such anguish.

We will revisit this later. He had six trials before several types of illegal gatherings; He was beaten and abused by the guards. On the fourth day, He was crucified. He became the consummate Paschal Lamb. He arrived in Jerusalem on the tenth Nissan and was crucified on the fourteenth Nissan. The light of Jesus' earthly life extinguished as He surrendered His Spirit. Four days after being welcomed by the Jewish people into His house in Jerusalem, He was crucified[11]. These four days symbolise the initial four days of creation. On the first day, He was introduced as spiritual light to the world while on the fourth day, He came to the earth as the 'Light of the World' amidst the darkness. This reflects the pattern of the first Passover Lamb. On day one, the lamb was invited into the home, and on day four, they killed it and used its blood for protection.

Death has been conquered, and He reigns over death and Hades. This truth is illustrated in Revelation 1:

'I am the Living One; I was dead, and now look, I am alive forever! And I hold the keys of death and Hades' (Rev. 1:18).

Three days later, He was raised from the dead and now sits at the Father's right hand, having completed His work. It is finished. This marks the first time He came. Jesus was raised from the dead and now holds power over death. He infiltrates Hades, takes dominion over that holding place, and delivers a significant blow to the powers and principalities in the heavens. You cannot enter a man's house before binding him. We will see how these last three days merge with the seven days of creation.

Returning to the family theme, Jesus was never separated from the Father. The Holy Spirit and Jesus are integral parts of God's family. For three hours on the cross, darkness enveloped the land. During this time, God placed the sins of the world upon Jesus, shrouding the land in darkness. He would not allow Jesus to be seen in this state. At the end of those three hours, Jesus cried out that God had forsaken Him. That was Jesus' separation from his family. God did not want to look upon His Son because of the sin laid upon Him. Separation from God is death. That is why I believe Jesus was troubled. It was this separation that concerned Him so. The torment of God, having to leave Him alone to satisfy His Holiness, stressed Jesus. Jesus cried out because His Father was not there for the first time. On the cross, He said, 'It is finished.' 'What is finished?' My companion posed another question.

The first Passover Lamb could not accomplish all that Jesus did; it provided protection only once. Additional sacrifices were necessary to maintain fellowship with God and sustain His presence among His people. This fellowship was at arm's length, mediated by a priest.

On the cross, Jesus fulfilled the sacrificial requirements of the Law of Moses; in His life, He obeyed the entire Law of Moses, after which the veil of the temple was torn apart. I will discuss this perfect life later as we follow His journey to the cross. His bodily death on the cross and His separation from the Father, which constituted actual death, satisfied the Holiness of God, and so it is finished.

However, that was not all. He went into the earth, where paradise was trapped, and freed all the Old

Testament Saints. We know He went to paradise because He told the thief on the cross, *'Today you will be with me in paradise.'* He did not say 'heaven.'

We also know from Matthew 27:53, but beginning at verse 50:

'And when Jesus had cried out again in a loud voice, he gave up his spirit' (Matt. 27:50).

Jesus gave up His Spirit after He said, 'It is finished.'

'At that moment, the temple curtain was torn in two from top to bottom. The earth shook, and the rocks split' (Matt. 27:51).

Jesus demolished the barrier of the vast curtain between man and God. He is now the way to the Father through His Body and Blood!

Hebrews 10 tells us:

'Therefore, brothers and sisters, since we have confidence to enter the Most Holy Place by the blood of Jesus, by a new and living way opened for us through the curtain, that is, his body' (Heb. 10:20).

There is no longer a barrier between man and God; we can now approach Him directly through Jesus—divine reconciliation. There is no need for temple sacrifices or priests. God, now satisfied, can dwell within us through

His Spirit, and we are living temples of our Holy God, with Jesus as our eternal High Priest.

The Holy Spirit serves as our guide in place of the Law, writing it on our hearts as we walk with Him. It is not the knowledge from the Tree of Good and Evil that directs us; instead, it is the Laws of God inscribed on our hearts by God, for we can never hope to accomplish that on our own. This constitutes a lifelong process of refinement.

But then, in the following verses of Matthew 27:50–52, we read:

And when Jesus had cried out again in a loud voice, he gave up his spirit. At that moment the curtain of the temple was torn in two from top to bottom. The earth shook, the rocks split and the tombs broke open. The bodies of many holy people who had died were raised to life (Matt. 27:50–52).

When Jesus was raised from the dead, the graves opened and those who had come out of the tombs went into Jerusalem, appearing to many. That must have shocked the family and friends who encountered what were, to them, deceased individuals. This would not have happened if these individuals had already been in Heaven. A Gentile centurion confirmed, 'This was the Son of God.' This aligns well with Paul's letter to the Ephesians, where he explains the believers' position in Christ in Ephesians 4:8. However, let us first turn to Psalm 68:18.

'When you ascended on high, you took many captives; you received gifts from people, even from the rebellious—that you, LORD God, might dwell there' (Ps. 68:18).

Paul quotes this in Ephesians 4:8:

'This is why it says: "When he ascended on high, he took many captives and gave gifts to his people"' (Eph. 4:8).

These captives were set free when the tombs were broken open, as in Matthew 27:53 and the following verse in Ephesians.

'(What does "he ascended" mean except that he also descended to the lower, earthly regions? He who descended is the very one who ascended higher than all the heavens to fill the whole universe)' (Eph. 4:9–10).

Numerous individuals have presented their interpretations of these verses. Nonetheless, I propose my perspective: Jesus arrived to dwell among us on Earth, and light permeated the world. No one can justly accuse God of establishing standards He could not fulfil. He descended to Earth, lived a life of perfection, and underwent a death without flaw. Subsequently, he descended further into the Earth when He proceeded to Paradise, referred to by the Hebrews as Abraham's Bosom—a holding place designated for the saints of the Old Testament.

The Gospel of Luke provides insight in Chapter Sixteen, into where paradise was, through the story of the 'Rich Man and Lazarus.' This is not a parable; it is Jesus informing us about life after death. The name Lazarus suggests he is 'God's helper'; it is not his poverty that allows him into paradise, but his faith in God.

Many stories told by Jesus are designated as parables, including the Parable of the Sower and the Seed, and the Parable of the Barren Fig Tree. This narrative features characters such as Abraham, Lazarus and the Rich Man, who engage in a conversation. The Rich Man, who did not know Abraham during his life, recognises him in death.

A parable represents a spiritual truth through an earthly illustration. Presently, there exists no earthly comparison for life after death. According to Jewish beliefs prevalent during that period, the souls of the deceased were gathered in a communal holding place. In the unseen world of the dead, the souls of the righteous occupied their abode, Abraham's Bosom, distinctly separated by a chasm from the abode assigned to the souls of the wicked in Hades.

The account in Luke reflects this concept. A gulf separated Paradise, or Abraham's Bosom, from the place of torment that no one could cross. This place of torment was in Hades, also known as Sheol, in the lower regions of the earth. You cannot enter a man's house without binding him and taking what you came for. Thus, Jesus descended into Paradise, as He had told the thief on the cross, and into the lower regions beneath the earth.

When Jesus descended, it was to free these captives in a place of rest called 'Abraham's Bosom;' they were not with God. As mentioned in Matthew 27:53, they were set free when the tombs were broken open. This was the second defeat of death; the first occurred when He was raised from the dead. This seals His rulership and declares His power as He now takes the 'Keys of Death and Hades.' When you have the keys to a door, you decide who comes and goes, granting you power.

He freed the captives and gained dominion over Death and Hades. The scarlet thread transforms to crimson. Four days after arriving in Jerusalem, He was crucified, and three days later, He rose from the dead. The heavenly forces have been defeated. Only three days remain until the seven-day redemption plan is fulfilled. During His return for these final three days, we will witness Jesus reclaiming authority over the physical world and lifting the earth's curse, a subject we will explore later.

His first arrival was just the beginning. Jesus is set to return a second time to defeat Satan, who has restricted access to Heaven and wanders the earth in a weakened state. This event will unfold in the final three days following the second harvest. It represents two days dedicated to Satan's defeat, with the seventh day marked by lifting the curse from the earth, as Jesus rules from Jerusalem during the millennium period. Let me clarify; stay with me!

Chapter Eleven - First Fruits Offering

The tombs were opened (Matthew 27:53). Although the other Gospels remain silent about this, it does not diminish its significance. Why did these individuals emerge from their tombs and enter Jerusalem? They were not zombies, devoid of speech or movement like robots; they were living, breathing people. If any of my deceased family members appeared at my door, I would be shocked, fearful and dumbfounded, but eventually joyous.

We must now examine why this has occurred. Jesus ascended to Heaven to present Himself as First Fruits to God. However, He took the barley harvest, or 'omer,' with Him—a significant leap. What is the connection to agriculture?

The Lord God established a routine for Israel to remember all He had done for them by providing a religious calendar. He first instituted the Sabbath day. They were to work for six days, and on the seventh day, they were to rest, just as God did during creation. From there, He set forth a series of seven memorial and prophetic feasts. The word used to describe a feast can also mean an appointed time. The number seven represents divine perfection.

The first feast is the Passover, commemorating God's deliverance of Israel from bondage in Egypt. However, it also looks forwards to Christ because, while it was a marvel and a miracle, the first Passover Lamb could only save once. They were to remember this event! Passover marks the beginning of the religious year. All feasts are reminders, but each one is also prophetic and unique, foreshadowing Christ, the Messiah.

The Seven Feasts of Israel start with the first four spring festivals.

- The Feast of Passover
- The Feast of Unleavened Bread
- The Feast of First Fruits
- The Feast of Pentecost (Weeks)

Jesus fulfilled the first phase of God's redemptive plan: a spiritual victory. Four days after entering Jerusalem, He was crucified. Three days later, He rose from the dead and secured victory over the powers and principalities in heavenly places.

The next three will be autumn festivals.

- The Blowing of Trumpets
- The Day of Atonement
- The Feast of Tabernacles

In this final phase, Jesus will reclaim His authority over the physical world upon His second coming. While discussing the significance of each feast would be interesting, it would divert us from our main topic. To summarise, these feasts represent a journey that spans from beginning to end, from the first to the last, and from death to life, mirroring the seven days of creation.

Leviticus 23 lists all the feasts God established and commanded the Israelites to keep. They are all extremely rich in prophetic meaning.

As a reminder, we are exploring why the tombs were opened when Jesus cried out and gave up His spirit, resulting in the Holy Ones emerging from them. The festivals, specifically the appointed times, are divided into spring and autumn. In Scripture, we see that when Jesus arrived, all the spring festivals were fulfilled.

- The Feast of Passover
- The Feast of Unleavened Bread
- **The Feast of First Fruits**
- The Feast of Pentecost (Weeks)

These spring festivals are reflected in the New Testament accounts of Jesus' life, death and resurrection. The Feast of First Fruits explains why these saints were set free and arose from their sleep. Additionally, these feasts serve as a pattern of redemption.

The Feast of First Fruits is a festival commanded by the Lord during the Passover celebration. It serves as a reminder to the Israelites of God's provision in the land. The Israelites are to recognise that God liberated them from slavery in Egypt and provided them with land to live and places to cultivate their crops. As a result, the Hebrew calendar became primarily a calendar for agricultural purposes.

The First Fruits Feast required the Israelites to bring a sheaf of the first grain (Hebrew: *omer*) from all the harvests, starting with barley, followed by wheat, and concluding with the final harvest of figs, olives and grapes at the end of the agricultural year. These offerings were to be presented to the priests before God (Leviticus 23:10). A sheaf is a bundle or cluster of the harvested grains.

The priest would take the bundle and wave it before the Lord on the day after the Sabbath. On that same day, all the Israelites were to sacrifice a year-old lamb without defect as a burnt offering and present a food offering of grain, oil and wine (Leviticus 23:11–13). The Israelites could not eat any of the crops until the day the first portion was presented to the High Priest. The first fruits belonged to God, and the people of Israel recognised Him as their provider (Leviticus 23:14).

Seven weeks following the Feast of First Fruits, the Israelites observed the Feast of Weeks, also called Pentecost. This is one of the three 'solemn feasts' that necessitate all Jewish males to make the journey to Jerusalem (Exodus 23:14–17; 34:22–23; Deuteronomy 16:16). Each of these important feasts required the presentation of the 'first fruits' from that specific harvest at the temple, corresponding to various crops.

This is the order.

The Feast of First Fruits, observed within Passover, specifically involved offering the first of the barley harvest.

The Feast of Weeks (Pentecost) offered the first wheat harvest.

The Feast of Tabernacles involved offering the first of the figs, olives and grape harvests.

Let us make a jump spiritually.

The Barley harvest—the spring harvest represents the first fruits from the Old Testament Saints.

First Fruits of the wheat harvest will be those born-again Christians harvested from spring through summer to autumn (the Church).

The figs, grapes and olives are then harvested in the autumn (those who pierced the Lord and will be future saints who survive the Tribulation).

Later, we will discuss how the figs, grapes and olives symbolise the Jews who recognise Jesus and are saved, while the others represent the Tribulation saints. For this to happen, Israel must be restored to its rightful place in the Land of Israel.

Let's return to the year's first harvest, which is barley. Barley is a lighter grain that ripens more quickly than wheat. It was the initial offering during the Feast of First Fruits in the Jewish agricultural calendar. In other words, the Feast of First Fruits celebrated the year's first harvest, reminding the Israelites of God's provision.

This was initiated so the Israelites would express gratitude to God for His provision after a long and labour-intensive crop-growing season. Since Ancient Israel was an agriculturally based society, the Israelites acknowledged God's provision for their food and income, marking the first step in the agricultural calendar.

Let us turn to 1 Corinthians 15, where Paul addresses those who deny the resurrection. They accepted the concept of life after death but suggested they would exist as spirit beings without physical bodies.

Paul must remind them of the gospel through which the Corinthians were saved and confirm that Christ is risen. He continues to discuss the order of the Resurrection.

'For as in Adam all die, so in Christ all will be made alive. But each in turn: Christ, the First fruits; then, when he comes, those who belong to him' (1 Cor. 15:22–23).

Old Testament saints belonged to Jesus. When Jesus died, He ascended to Heaven to offer Himself as the First Fruits. But what would be this fruit? He needed to bring part of the harvest with Him. Since the Church had not yet materialised—that would not occur for another 50 days—He had to take a gift with Him. Remember, He is the great High Priest, and just like the High Priest under the Law of Moses, He needed to wave an offering ('omer') before God.

This 'omer' was held in Paradise in the lower regions of the earth, yet separate from the Father because the Blood had not yet been given. Therefore, paradise used to be in the lower regions of the earth, but now it exists in Heaven. These Old Testament saints represented the 'omer' offering. Today, we assume that paradise exists in Heaven; however, there was a time when it was in the Earth, and not where God resides, in the third heaven. It could not be so, as innocent blood had not yet been spilt.

Elijah and Enoch are the exception, but whether they were taken to the third heaven, where God resides, remains unclear. This seems unlikely because Jesus had not yet died and offered His Blood in the Holy of Holies.

Old Testament saints remained in Abraham's Bosom until the blood of Christ set them free. It could not be otherwise; Jesus had not yet died. They never earned the right to be with God in Heaven. Without the precious, innocent human blood being taken to the Holy of Holies in the Heavenly Tabernacle, no human being could be with our Lord.

Luke chapter 16 alludes to this when the rich man speaks with Abraham. He is in a place of torment while Lazarus is with Abraham. There is no place of torment where God resides in Heaven.

Back to Matthew 27:53. The tombs were opened, and those who emerged from their graves were part of the Barley Harvest that Christ presented as the first fruits from the dead to God. Paul also informed us that paradise is now in the third heaven. Paul relates his vision and the thorn God gave him to suppress vanity and pride. But he says in 2 Corinthians 12:2–4:

I know a man in Christ who fourteen years ago was caught up to the third heaven. Whether it was in the body or out of the body I do not know—God knows. And I know that this man—whether in the body or apart from the body I do not know, but God knows—was caught up to paradise and heard inexpressible things, things that no one is permitted to tell (2 Cor. 12:2–4).

Paul discusses a near-death experience he likely had years earlier while he was stoned and left for dead, as recounted in Acts 14. In verse 2, he mentions being caught up to the third heaven, the dwelling place of the Lord, and in verse 4, he asserts that he was taken up to paradise.

While this chapter is fascinating, I will refrain from discussing it here. Paradise now resides with God in the third heaven. When Jesus ascended, He brought those who were captive in the earth, where paradise once existed, and carried all of paradise to Heaven as the First Fruits of the Barley Harvest, the Old Testament saints. Their lives and adherence to the Law of Moses could never fulfil God's requirements.

Chapter Twelve - Pentecost

Next, Pentecost is equivalent to 'The Feast of Weeks,' as described in the Jewish festival year outlined in Leviticus 23: The Feast of Weeks is the second of the three 'solemn feasts' that all Jewish males were required to travel to Jerusalem to attend (Exodus 23:14–17; 34:22–23; Deuteronomy 16:16). This vital feast is named after the seven complete weeks, or precisely fifty days, following the Feast of First Fruits. Because it occurs exactly fifty days after the previous feast, this celebration is also known as 'Pentecost' (Acts 2:1), which means 'fifty.'

This was also when the Holy Spirit, Christ's gift to us from His Father, was fulfilled as promised by Jesus due to His perfect sacrifice (Acts 2:1–4.) In Peter's sermon, which describes the remarkable events when the Holy Spirit descended, verse 41 states that 3,000 people believed.

The day the Holy Spirit came marked the birth of the Church. You will see later that He is Jesus' wedding gift to us. They will represent the wheat harvest collected at the end of summer when we are taken out of this world. In the Old Testament, the Holy Spirit was bestowed only upon God's anointed for ministry or service, and He could be withdrawn for rebellion or gross immorality.

As temples of the Holy Spirit, we are assured that He will always remain with those devoted to Christ, as we are betrothed to Him. Upon Jesus' return to gather us from the earth, we will be presented as part of the wheat harvest. I will later discuss how this connects to our betrothal and rapture through the Last Supper. Some argue against the rapture, believing the Church must endure the Great Tribulation. However, how can a groom permit His bride to suffer?

Teachers should educate based on the following principles: context, culture and audience. Let us reflect on the life of our Lord. When He preached and taught, He did so among the Jews, particularly the Galileans. Much of the Gospels' content unfolded along the shores of the Sea of Galilee. Therefore, when we teach or preach the Bible, we must consider all three aspects and never teach outside this safety net. This principle applies to the entirety of God's Word. **Context, Culture and Audience.**

Chapter Thirteen - The Autumn of the World

Genesis 1 is an account of creation and redemption. God created it in seven days, even though He could have done it instantly.

We then focused on the first day of creation and the light God brought into the world. Jesus, the light of the world, shines in the darkness. On the fourth day, God illuminated the earth through the heavens and their stars, symbolising Jesus' arrival, and the light He brings to humanity by revealing the Father to us.

God is purposeful and never makes mistakes. He represents law and order, establishing unchangeable laws for Heaven and Earth. Within His Word, He has intricately crafted mysteries for humanity to uncover with His assistance over time. The Bible reveals mysteries but holds no secrets. Secrets are hidden and not intended for revelation. Nations, individuals and countries maintain secrets for various reasons; they prefer to keep their possessions, actions and plans undisclosed. The Bible serves a purpose: it guides individuals to uncover a truth under Heaven that embodies God's plan for them, enabling us to live in communion with Him while ultimately upholding His holiness. It is rich in mysteries but devoid of secrets.

'I make known the end from the beginning, from ancient times, what is still to come. I say, "My purpose will stand, and I will do all that I please."' (Isa. 46:10).

Creation, the first Passover, and Jesus' death are all interconnected in the creation narrative, forming a crimson thread of redemption that is often barely visible. Time began 'in the beginning' in Genesis 1, taking seven days to create the heavens, the earth and life. Four days are mentioned when the Hebrews were commanded to keep a lamb in their households to protect against impending death.

The lamb was brought into the Israelites' homes on day one and was killed on day four. This first Passover Lamb, commanded by God, was sacrificed so that its blood would protect the Israelites from the Lord (Exodus 11:4–5). God killed the firstborn who were not covered by this blood. Many people may not appreciate its portrayal in such blunt terms. However, God does not share our sensibilities. Death and life are alike to Him. Those He kills today can live again if He chooses. His choices are based on His Holiness. We must rid ourselves of this feeble, liberal and overly nice view of God and fear the one who holds the Keys to death and Hades, while remembering that He is also full of grace, mercy, love and died for us!

Jesus was crucified four days after reaching Jerusalem, and three days later, he rose from the dead. On the first day of creation, he was introduced as the Light of the World in the darkness, while on the fourth day, God created the celestial bodies to illuminate the earth. Thus, Jesus entered our world as the Light of the World and defeated the heavenly forces of evil.

He now rests, for His work of salvation is complete. Four days after being welcomed into Jerusalem, the same people who greeted Him allowed His execution despite His innocence. One of the thieves on the cross declared Him blameless. Jesus rose on the third day, which the first Passover Lamb could not do. However, our Lord is not yet finished. Creation itself must be granted rest from the curse of sin. He must return to accomplish this, in the 'Autumn of the World.'

Chapter Fourteen - As a Thief in the Night

This chapter might also be named, 'No One Knows the Day, Nor the Hour.' The church appears ambivalent regarding Jesus' return. His death, resurrection and ascension to Heaven are key milestones in the story. Nevertheless, few church leaders prioritise teaching their congregations about His imminent return. The church focuses on holy living, discipleship, testimonies and evangelism. While these elements are essential, the significance of prophetic teachings in the Bible must not be overlooked. Prophecy offers hope, and the prophecies in the Bible are meant to encourage the Church to look up. However, we wander like beasts, burdened by heavy loads; few proclaim, 'Look up, for your redemption is near.'

Understanding Jesus' message about His return is vital; read Matthew 24, Mark 13 and Luke 21. When discussing His return, you often encounter scepticism, as if people think, 'Oh, he is one of those.' The Evangelists are diligently spreading the word. Many are finding their way into the kingdom, and across the globe we see signs of people coming to know our Lord. I wish there were even more, but the Holy Spirit is actively at work. With His guidance, we strive to lead them into the kingdom, proclaim the gospel and reinforce the message, but are they left with eternal hope? Although we may speak of Jesus' return, we often fail to offer substantial teachings that foster faith; many leaders, elders and vicars hesitate to address this topic.

When I started teaching Revelation, I quickly noticed that members viewed it as merely spiritual warfare, something to be overlooked. This viewpoint was shaped by what they had previously heard. Unfortunately, few churches take the time to explore prophecy. Many valuable insights go untaught since a significant third of the Bible is prophetic. Although Revelation can be startling, it is meant to inspire us; it encompasses much more than just the spiritual aspect.

Let us continue our exploration with another mystery as anticipation grows. We have examined Jesus' first coming and recognise that He will return. How can we reconcile this with statements like 'no one knows the day nor the hour' or 'a thief in the night'? Is this about His second coming, or should we anticipate something different? The Bible cites specific timeframes concerning the end. Thus, while the date of Jesus' second coming can be pinpointed, it can only be discerned by those alive during that period, particularly those who will endure the Great Tribulation mentioned in Revelation.

We will discuss individuals who think they are saved but remain after the rapture later. In Revelation chapters 11 and 12, the author John alludes to a timeframe of 1,260 days associated with two prophecies concerning the persecution of Jews during the end times. Daniel notes three specific timeframes: 2,300 days, 1,290 days and 1,335 days. Now, let's delve deeper into this subject.

We see the mountain peak ahead, so we must look back to anticipate what may be ahead. The Bible mentions 2,300 days in a prophecy by Daniel concerning the persecution of the Jewish people, spanning the period between the Old and New Testaments. This prophecy was fulfilled precisely when the temple was desecrated before the birth of Christ, during the reign of the Seleucid king, Antiochus IV (Epiphanes). He states that the temple will be desecrated. Research indicates that Antiochus desecrated the temple in Jerusalem and severely persecuted the Jews from September 171/170 BC to December 165/164 BC.

Then I heard a holy one speaking, and another holy one said to him, "How long will it take for the vision to be fulfilled—the vision concerning the daily sacrifice, the rebellion that causes desolation, the surrender of the sanctuary and the trampling underfoot of the LORD's people?" He said to me, "It will take 2,300 evenings and mornings; then the sanctuary will be reconsecrated" (Dan. 8:13–14).

When Antiochus died, the Jews purified and rededicated the temple, just as Daniel had predicted. These events are commemorated in the Jewish celebration of Hanukkah and were fulfilled to the very day! If a prophet prophesies and that prophecy comes to pass, that person is of God! After reflecting on Daniel, let us focus on the other prophetic days mentioned in two passages of Revelation that are still unfulfilled. The first is found in Revelation 11:3, which states:

'And I will appoint my two witnesses, and they will prophesy for 1,260 days, clothed in sackcloth' (Rev. 11:3).

This remains unfulfilled; if you witnessed two men of God performing signs and wonders as described in Revelation 11:3–12, you would have to be blind not to see the significance of those days. People would have their devices recording these events. The detailed prophecies in God's Word contribute to the Bible's uniqueness among religious texts. Our God can "make known the end from the beginning, from ancient times, what is still to come" (Isaiah 46:10), and He has revealed significant future events, counting the very days of those periods.

How do you compare those specific days when Jesus says, 'No one knows the day nor the hour'? I can understand not knowing the hour. However, we could determine the day if Jerusalem were being trampled and a peace treaty were being broken, as alluded to in Daniel 9:27. We will address this chapter of Daniel later. Indeed, it does not relate to 'like a thief in the night.'

Let us clarify and show that Jesus' reference to not knowing 'the day nor the hour' in Matthew 24 does not relate to His second coming.

'But about that day or hour no one knows, not even the angels in Heaven, nor the Son, but only the Father. As it was in the days of Noah, so it will be at the coming of the Son of Man' (Matt. 24:37).

Before the flood, Jesus ensured Noah's safety so he would not endure what the world would experience.

'For in the days before the flood, people were eating and drinking, marrying, and giving in marriage, up to the day Noah entered the ark' (Matt. 24:38).

Noah boarded the Ark, and his actions did not go unnoticed. It took him more than a century to build this vessel, and it was hardly a secret. Erecting such a large structure on a mountain far from water would have caught attention. People likely mocked and derided him for suggesting that God would flood the earth. How would Noah get that enormous ship to the sea?

'And they knew nothing about what would happen until the flood came and took them all away. That is

how it will be at the coming of the Son of Man' (Matt. 24:39).

When Jesus comes for the Church, this is how it will be. Let us read on.

Two men will be in the field; one will be taken and the other left. Two women will be grinding with a hand mill; one will be taken and the other left. Therefore keep watch, because you do not know what day your Lord will come (Matt 24:40–42).

As Jesus indicates in these verses, people will vanish when He returns for His church. This will not happen amid major global disasters, similar to those mentioned in Revelation 6–19, but somewhat parallels Noah's experience. God rescues His believers from the judgement awaiting those who reject Christ, much like He saved Noah. It is only after the Church is removed that Satan will be unleashed. Once the Church leaves Earth and the Holy Spirit stands aside, the man of sin will emerge.

If you find yourself left on Earth, God forbid, you possess the information needed to navigate the day. Those who believed they were safe but were left behind can look to God's word for guidance. Jesus Himself says He will return. I believe He will come back once to gather His church, and later, at the end of the Great Tribulation period outlined in Revelation 6–19,

He will arrive with an army for all to see. This event will signify His second coming. Thieves in the night do not reveal their plans.

When He comes for us, His people, we will ascend to meet Him in the air. Unlike the depiction in Revelation 19 of His arrival on a white horse with armies, we will instead greet Him in the clouds. When He comes for His church, one will be taken and another left. This will be a silent arrival, not the bang, crash and horror of the seven seals, trumpets and bowls of God's anger mentioned in Revelation.

Let us clarify this further! The story of Jesus' ascension is genuinely fascinating. Can you imagine what happens as Jesus ascends into Heaven? He shares this incredible moment with His disciples, as seen in Luke 24:50–51 and Acts 1:10–11:

'When he had led them out to the vicinity of Bethany, he lifted his hands and blessed them. While he was blessing them, he left them and was taken up into heaven' (Luke 24:50–51).

'After he said this, he was taken up before their very eyes, and a ***cloud*** *hid him from their sight. They were looking intently up into the sky as he was going when suddenly two men dressed in white stood beside them'* (Acts 1:9–10).

These were angels.

'"Men of Galilee," they said, "Why do you stand here looking into the sky? This same Jesus, who has been taken from you into Heaven, ***will come back in the same way you have seen him go into heaven****"'* (Acts 1:11).

The angels declared that just as you witnessed Him ascending, you will also see Him return. Consequently, Jesus will come back on clouds in the sky, just like He ascended, rather than on a white horse with an army of heaven filled with all majesty and sound. Jesus ascends by His authority, without a white horse or an army, simply in a cloud, observed by the men of Galilee, His followers. When He returns, He will beckon us from the clouds to join Him. After he left, the Church began to grow. He will return in the same way—not on a white horse as in Revelation 19— but to take us to Heaven on a cloud, and people will disappear. To confirm this, we will refrain from referencing the typical verses about the Church's rapture; we will examine it through the lens of the Last Supper, the creation of a New Covenant in His Blood and a betrothal.

Chapter Fifteen - A Galilean Wedding

This chapter draws inspiration from the documentary *Before the Wrath* (Ingenuity Films). Jay McCarl, a distinguished author and theologian, contributed his expertise to the film through his book *Best Day Forever*[11]. However, the documentary, in certain segments, has been dramatised, and elements of the wedding ceremony have been staged for effect. Ancient wedding customs throughout the Middle East were varied. The Bible does not specify explicit procedures for marriage. Jewish wedding traditions, spanning from the Old Testament era to the time of Jesus, are abundant with diverse customs. The dramatisation of the wedding ceremony within the documentary is solely intended for dramatic purposes.

After analysing the various rituals involved, I have elected to concentrate on the principal theme presented in the documentary. In numerous cultural traditions, the bride and groom exchange cups. In some Jewish wedding customs, the 'hora' is a circular dance that culminates with the bride and groom being lifted into the air on chairs after sharing the cups—another tradition symbolising celebration for the couple and performed after the betrothal. This 'lifting' portrays the moment of our union with Christ in the clouds.

The section about the 'Flight of the Bride' highlights some regional customs, though it isn't seen as a standard practice. After reflecting on this and considering how the writer, Brent Miller Jr., portrays the wedding, I believe that the core of the dramatisation effectively symbolises our Betrothal to Jesus and our future marriage to Christ, as referenced in Revelation 19:7 (NKJV). In verse 7, we are called His wife; we became His wife during the Last Supper when we shared a cup.

No extra-biblical evidence is required for the 'rapture of the Church' because the Bible is its authority and the evidence is there. Let me qualify this.

- Jesus refers to Himself as a bridegroom (Matthew 9:15)
- We share a cup at the Last Supper, as in a Jewish wedding
- The wedding covenant is established at the Last Supper
- Jesus arrives for us as previously described, when we are ascended to heaven as He summons us from the clouds. This process is akin to guiding a bride to her new residence.
- A marriage supper happens in heaven (Revelation 19), and after this, Jesus 'Second Coming' happens later in Revelation 19

Considering all these factors and reflecting on the themes discussed in the film, as shared by writer and director Brent Miller Jr, was truly inspiring.

There is considerable criticism regarding the accuracy of this documentary; however, such critiques primarily originate from individuals who do not believe in the rapture of the church.

We will analyse The Last Supper, but removing culture and audience from this context diminishes its prophetic perspective. Many elements of Jesus' actions during the Last Supper would have been clear to His disciples; they'd have understood and needed no further explanation. While looking into The Last Supper, I named this chapter 'A Galilean Wedding.' Let us spark our imagination. To help with this, let me introduce the main characters. We are progressing swiftly now!

- Bride and Bridegroom
- Both fathers of the couple
- Elders at the gate
- Immediate family
- Witnesses

In ancient biblical times, individuals often entered matrimony at a young age, with such unions typically arranged among close family or social circles. Marriage outside these circles was generally discouraged due to differing beliefs and customs. Fathers primarily facilitated the arrangements, while daughters were often consulted about their opinions. The main concern focused more on sons than on daughters. No financial obligations were incurred regarding the marriage of a daughter. Originally, the dowry (mohar) represented the bride's purchase price; when she left her father's home, a valuable pair of hands was lost. In ancient times, marriage was not merely a union between individuals but a significant bond between families. This event was important enough to draw most villagers and townspeople to attend.

To be considered legal and ratified, the ceremony must occur in a visible location in front of the village, attended by town elders and witnesses. Key participants include the bridegroom, the bride and the witnesses. The Rabbi's role is to facilitate the ceremony and ensure adherence to Jewish law. A Galilean wedding is intricately connected to the Last Supper as a betrothal. This ancient Galilean wedding custom anticipates the reality of the rapture.

Both Jews and Gentiles referred to the inhabitants of the region north of Judea as Galileans. The residents of this area were known by the term 'Galilee of the Gentiles' (Isaiah 9:1, Matt 4:15) or, more accurately, 'the District of the Gentiles.' Although Jewish and devoted to Israel, the people in this area were regarded by their compatriots to the south as somewhat inferior (**context**).

Judeans often regarded Galileans with disdain, viewing them as uneducated and of dubious ancestry (John 1:46;

7:52). Galileans had gained a reputation for being troublemakers, as they were frequently involved in protests and uprisings against the Roman occupiers. Jesus grew up in Galilee (Matthew 2:19–23) and gathered his first disciples there when he launched his ministry and performed his initial miracles (Matthew 4:17–23; John 2:11). Consequently, they were Galilean Jews (**audience**).

Jesus began His ministry in Galilee. He 'was despised and held in low esteem' (Isaiah 53:3). Zealots arose from this region, and Pharisaism thrived among the hill people of Galilee. Jesus came to these Jews. We will examine Jewish weddings, particularly those from Galilee (**culture**).

The Betrothal

In this timeframe, a wedding emerged as the most important event for the entire town. People hurried to the betrothal at the main gate, where witnesses held just as much significance as the guests. Here, the bride is offered a proposal with a covenant and gifts are shared. The main gate or another central spot frequently became a gathering place for elders and leaders to engage in various business transactions, both formal and informal.

Before we continue, we need to gather relevant scriptures for this ceremony. Let us examine the passage in which Jesus addresses His disciples regarding the end times. In Matthew 24:32, Jesus advises the disciples to be vigilant for these signs: 'Now learn this parable from the fig tree.' The Lord teaches us a spiritual lesson through nature. Summer is approaching when the fig tree branches become green and tender. In the Bible, the fig tree has historically symbolised Israel. Shortly after this, Jesus states concerning an event:

'But about that day or hour no one knows, not even the angels in heaven, nor the Son, but only the Father' (Matt. 24:36).

Remember that verse. The following verse we need is from John 14:1. The context is that just before this, at the end of John 13, Jesus informed His disciples He would be betrayed and He would be leaving, specifically telling Peter he would deny Him. This news troubled the disciples, but Jesus reassured them in the first four verses.

Do not let your hearts be troubled. You believe in God; believe also in me. My Father's house has many rooms; if that were not so, would I have told you that I am going there to prepare a place for you? ***And if I go and prepare a place for you, I will come back and take you to be with me that you also may be where I am.*** *You know the way to the place where I am going* (John 14:1–4).

He goes to prepare a home for them. Commit this to memory. The following verses come from the Last

Supper; let us turn to Matthew 26:26–29. This is also recorded in the other Gospels.

While they were eating, Jesus took bread, and when he had given thanks, he broke it and gave it to his disciples, saying, 'Take and eat; this is my body.' ***Then he took a cup, and when he had given thanks, he gave it to them, saying, 'Drink from it, all of you. This is my blood of the covenant, which is poured out for many for the forgiveness of sins'*** (Matt. 26:26–28).

In this passage, the Lord introduces the New Covenant. This covenant will evolve into the New Way after Jesus fulfils the Mosaic Covenant and its stipulations. The Law given to Moses remains in effect, but it is fulfilled, and God was pleased with Jesus. When you have a covenant or agreement with someone, fulfilling its terms means it ceases to bind you. Like a financial contract, paying off the debt releases you from its obligation. This New Covenant would be sealed in His blood, and the bread would represent His body. To combat a disease, one must go to ground zero. Adam was ground zero and Christ is the antidote. The disease no longer exists for those who take the medicine. A person is either under the Law or under Grace.

But look at what He says in verse 29:

'I tell you; I will not drink from this fruit of the vine from now on until that day when I drink it new with you in my Father's kingdom' (Matt. 26:29).

We will circle back to that later! Let us shine a light on the disciples and their worries about His departure. Jesus reassures them by promising to send a helper who will be with them and guide them along the way.

'But when the Spirit of truth comes, ***He will guide you into all the truth.*** *He will not speak on his own; He will speak only what he hears and tell you what is yet to come'* (John 16:13).

All these scriptures converge in the Galilean Wedding. While we delve into the wedding ceremony, remember that it is a significant event for Jews and particularly important to Galileans. The wedding day is announced, and the wedding party features the bride, the groom and their fathers. The ceremony encompasses various phases in different Jewish communities, with contemporary betrothals having developed over time. However, during Jesus' era in Galilee, the ceremony involved a covenant, an oath and a wedding feast. At the Last Supper, Jesus assumes the role of the groom, with His disciples as His betrothed. The witnesses include the Father, His Holy Spirit and the angels.

The bride and groom primarily wear white. If they had the means, they would prefer luxurious white linen. Their wedding attire would resemble elegant, full-length bathrobes with distinctive designs. He would don unique headwear while she would wear a veil.

This reminds me of the high priest's attire on a remarkable occasion—Yom Kippur, the Day of

Atonement, one of the feasts that God commanded Israel to observe.

During this sacred celebration, the High Priest replaces his traditional non-white attire (Exodus 28). The vivid purple and crimson robes usually worn by the High Priest and the Tabernacle's inner colour scheme allow him to maintain an understated presence within our Lord's dwelling, preventing him from overshadowing the surroundings.

At the same time, the reflective stones representing the twelve tribes of Israel embedded in the garment do not align with the colour scheme of the Holy of Holies and shine brightly. On Yom Kippur, when He offers the blood and enters the Holy of Holies with it, he is dressed in fine white linen (Ketonet)—a symbol of purity (Lev. 16:4). Our bride and groom would wear fine white linen at the betrothal if they could afford it.

The ceremony consists of two parts: the betrothal, and the second occurs in the future when all conditions are met. In Middle Eastern and Jewish cultures, the second part, the wedding feast, is usually held about a year after the betrothal.

At this point, both fathers face each other while the bride and groom stand beside them, gazing at one another for everyone to witness. The groom's father reads the covenant agreement aloud, which significantly favours the bride, and the groom readily accepts the responsibilities that come with it. Once the covenant and responsibilities are read aloud and accepted, they become a legal agreement establishing the resulting bond.

Next, the father reaches for a cup known as the '**Cup of Joy**' to seal the agreement. The groom's father hands the cup to his son. After receiving the cup, a pitcher of wine is given to him. He fills the cup with wine and then turns to his bride. This moment can be challenging because, although the families have approved it, the bride still holds the most power. The groom presents the bride with the **'Cup of Joy'** that is filled with wine. The bride then has the authority to accept or decline the offer. For the wedding to proceed, the bride must drink from this cup.

Given their Galilean background, the disciples doubtless grasped the situation. The groom offers the cup to the bride, who can accept it or hand it back. If she decides to hand it back for any reason, the marriage is over. At this moment, she takes the cup, drinks from it and returns it to the overjoyed groom. He lifts the '**Cup of Joy'** high and shows it to the crowd. Drinking from the cup, he shouts with excitement and confirms the moment with this:

'You are now consecrated to me by the laws of Moses, and I will not drink from this cup again until I drink it with you in my father's house.'

Jesus' statement is subtly different. The groom at the wedding swears by the Law of Moses to seal this covenant, as oaths are often binding by invoking a higher authority. In this context, the Law of Moses was the ultimate authority in Jewish culture and tradition. However, Jesus holds the highest authority. During the Last Supper, He affirms the covenant with His blood, which He ultimately offers to God upon entering the Holy of Holies in the third heaven; importantly, He does not invoke the Law of Moses.

A dowry is exchanged. Although initially this was the purchase price of the bride (mohar), the bride's parents could also contribute (Aramaic, Nedunya).

The tradition of giving a dowry is rooted in ancient customs. Daughters typically did not inherit from their fathers' estates. Upon marriage, their parents would provide a dowry, intending to offer her as much security as they could afford. Her husband managed her dowry as part of the family assets. In the event of a divorce without cause, a man was required to return the dowry his wife had brought with her as part of the bride price. This arrangement protected the bride, as her removal would incur significant costs. If the woman died childless, her dowry reverted to her father and family. Importantly, if her husband died, she would still have the means to live. The dowry bestowed by our heavenly Father provides us with security for the future. At the Last Supper, this dowry from the Father held immense value. It was His Son who assured us of a future with God. Jesus was the Father's gift to us.

The Last Supper (John 13)

Jesus offered His disciples a cup of wine at the Last Supper, symbolising a New Covenant.

After the disciples drink from the cup (Matthew 26:29), Jesus says similar words to the tradition of the groom from the Ancient Galilean wedding, **'But I say to you, I will not drink of this fruit of the vine from now on, until that day that I drink it with you in my Father's kingdom.'**

This cup given to His disciples signifies a New Covenant. He would pour His blood and invite them to participate in this union. Jesus spoke as a bridegroom during the Last Supper, and the disciples understood the moment's significance.

Note that gifts are given to the bride from the bridegroom!

Chapter Sixteen - The Wedding Feast

Now that the first part of the ceremony is complete, both parties must prepare for the next phase. In many cultures, the second part of the wedding is a banquet traditionally celebrated over seven days. Both the groom and the bride have much to do.

As I mentioned, it takes about a year from the wedding date to the wedding feast. The family sets dates so everyone knows how much time remains for preparations. The bride had to prepare herself, which was not easy in those days. Jewish law establishes the wedding dates they can set according to specific rules. It cannot be held during festivals such as Yom Kippur, Passover, the Sabbath or even the Days of Preparation.

According to Jewish texts, Tuesday is regarded as an auspicious day, symbolising the third day of creation. In the narrative of Creation, Tuesday is uniquely distinguished as the only day where the Torah asserts 'Good' twice: 'And God saw that it was good.' In the broader context of Jewish weddings, a specific date is generally established, typically ranging from six months to a year. The families consent to this arrangement to guarantee that preparations can be adequately made on both sides.

The wedding date is flexible, with preparations contingent upon the bride's eventual residence. The father of the groom will determine when he is satisfied, typically allowing a lead time of six months to a year

'But about that day or hour no one knows, not even the angels in heaven, nor the Son, but only the Father. As it was in the days of Noah, so it will be at the coming of the Son of Man' (Matt. 24:36–37).

No warning is given. The great tribulation and destruction leading up to Jesus' second coming are not like a thief in the night. However, we observe life continuing here.

For in the days before the flood, people were eating and drinking, marrying, and giving in marriage, up to the day Noah entered the ark; and they knew nothing about what would happen until the flood came and took them all away. That is how it will be at the coming of the Son of Man (Matt. 24:38–39).

The bride understood it would take at least a year so she needed to prepare. She could travel, but going out alone was not permitted.

And I will ask the Father, and ***he will give you another advocate to help you and be with you forever****—the*

Spirit of truth. The world cannot accept him because it neither sees nor knows him. But you know him; he lives with you and will be in you (John 14:16–17).

That was precisely the case at the Galilean wedding. As the bride, what present did we receive at His ascension?

'I will not leave you as orphans*; I will come to you'* (John 14:18).

In ancient Jewish culture, a betrothed woman was legally married to a man but remained in her father's home until the wedding feast. She would not be allowed to go out on her own. The betrothal ceremony, known as kiddushin, marked the initial step in a two-part process that created a legal bond between the couple.

When Jesus ascended to Heaven, He requested a helper from the Father, who granted us a companion to aid in our wedding preparations after we accept the cup of salvation. The Holy Spirit is our precious gift, assisting us like the bride's companions who are always by her side, allowing her the freedom to prepare for her new life as she is united in marriage. The Holy Spirit represents our engagement ring and our tiara! He also bestows upon us the gifts of the Spirit. The Father sends His Spirit to live within us and provides guardian angels for our protection! He resides in us and guides us.

There were no wedding planners or shops to visit. The bride may have had to travel far and wide to fulfil her needs for this event. Traditionally, the groom would arrive at midnight, so the unmarried bridesmaids needed lamps to light the way for the groom and the wedding party. When they eventually arrived, the light from these lamps guided the procession. She feels safe during her travels to gather her supplies, knowing that trusted companions care for her.

In the ancient tradition of Galilean weddings, after the betrothal, the groom departs to his father's house to arrange the wedding feast. The lavishness of the celebration depends on the family and the father's resources. While the feast holds great significance, the location where the groom prepares for his bride is equally vital. The bride is not abandoned; Jesus has given us His gift from the Father.

Our trusted **companion,** the Holy Spirit!

Chapter Seventeen - The Flight of the Bride

The groom prepares for her.

Following the betrothal, the groom is expected to fulfil his responsibilities. He goes back to his father's house and traditionally adds an extension.

My Father's house has many rooms; if that were not so, would I have told you that I am going there to prepare a place for you? ***And if I go and prepare a place for you, I will come back and take you to be with me that you also may be where I am*** (John 14:2–3).

Everything is coming together. The project requires resources he cannot obtain from a local builder's merchant. If his father has land with the necessary resources, he can source them locally; otherwise, he may need to look elsewhere. He needs workers and skilled artisans to help build the extension, the perfect place for a perfect bride.

Preparing the wedding feast involves organising the food, cooking arrangements, and gifts for the bride, her bridesmaids and family. This important task demands considerable lead time ahead of the ceremony. A designated area for the bride will be furnished with new furniture, tables and stools, while the wedding feast will showcase oil lamps and rugs in the new home.

When he feels ready, the groom approaches his father to seek permission to take his bride; however, his father responds, 'Not yet, my son.' Nevertheless, the father is already contemplating a date that will align with when he is satisfied that the residence his son has constructed is suitable for his bride and that the wedding preparations are finalised, ensuring accommodation for all guests. Moreover, he must consider the season, as neither **autumn nor winter** would be acceptable.

The son is excited as he senses the moment drawing near to get his bride. Meanwhile, the workers busily construct the bride's litter, designed like a chair with poles on either side, ready to carry this precious cargo to his father's house, just like a palanquin. Once the litter is completed, he returns to his father, who softly replies, 'Not yet.' Still, the son can feel that the season will change soon and knows it is almost time. Then, not long after, at midnight, the father gently awakens his son to share the wonderful news that the moment they have been waiting for has finally arrived. Overjoyed, the son eagerly tells his companions, 'He obtains a shofar (trumpet).' He joyfully sounds the horn and continues with the 'Trump.'

This echoes 1 Thessalonians 1:4, where Paul speaks of the final trumpet call; however, he must clarify that their perception of life after death is incorrect. They held the belief in a universal resurrection and a final judgement. However, Paul asserts:

'According to the Lord's word, we tell you that we who are still alive, who are left until the coming of the Lord, will certainly not precede those who have fallen asleep' (1 Thess. 4:15).

The correction starts:

'For the Lord himself will come down from heaven, with a loud command, with the voice of the archangel and with the trumpet call of God, and the dead in Christ will rise first' (1 Thess. 4:16).

Jesus calls His Bride.

After that, we who are still alive and are left will be caught up together with them ***in the clouds*** *to meet the Lord in the air. And so, we will be with the Lord forever. Therefore, encourage one another with these words* (1 Thess. 4:17–18).

Those who belong to the Lord and are alive on Earth at this time will ascend and join Him in the 'clouds,' just as the angel told the disciples in Acts 1:11. Paul indicates that these are the words of the Lord Himself.

The groom strolls through the village, blowing the Shofar. The guests, eagerly anticipating this moment, awaken to its sound. They hear the trumpet's call and prepare themselves, ever watchful for signals, knowing the time is near because the season is right.

The excitement starts as the bride and her bridesmaids hear the trumpet's call. They prepare their lamps, already filled with oil, which blaze brightly as the bride gets ready. She steps to the door, waiting eagerly as she notices the lights in the distance. The bridesmaids create a procession to lead the wedding party to the bride's home as the night is completely dark—there were no street lamps then.

The groom stands in his stunning white wedding attire. His face lights up with a broad smile as he sees his bride, and he excitedly gestures toward the bride's litter. She elegantly lowers herself onto her chair, which is lifted into the air, symbolising the moment He comes for us. The journey takes the bride from her father's house to her father-in-law's house. This part of the ceremony is known as '**The Flight of the Bride**.' Upon arrival at his father's house, the wedding party invites all guests to join the celebration. Once everyone is inside, the doors are closed to prohibit further entry.

In contrast to Jesus' second coming, let us go to Revelation 19.

I saw heaven standing open, and there before me was a white horse, whose rider is called Faithful and True.

With justice, he judges and wages war. His eyes are like blazing fire, and on his head are many crowns. He has a name written on him that no one knows but himself (Rev. 19:11–12).

This is a king ready for judgement, *not* a groom coming for His Bride.

'He is dressed in a robe dipped in blood, and his name is the Word of God. The armies of Heaven were following him, riding on white horses and dressed in fine linen, white and clean' (Rev. 19:13–14).

His bride is dressed in fine white linen. Note the emphasis on 'those following' were also white and clean.

'Coming out of his mouth is a sharp sword to strike down the nations. *"He will rule them with an iron sceptre." He treads the winepress of the fury of the wrath of God Almighty'* (Rev. 19:15).

This is not like a thief in the night. In reaction, the earth prepares to fight against our Lord. The beast and the false prophet are cast into the lake of fire and Satan is confined for a thousand years. When Jesus returns for His bride, 'one will be taken and the other left.' This refers to **'The Flight of the Bride**.' Quietly and calmly, people will disappear like thieves in the night. At this point, my companion reminded me of the first miracle Jesus performed. It was at a wedding!

Chapter Eighteen – Wise and Foolish Virgins

From this point, the weaving of scripture becomes intricate and may require considerable meditation. Persist and you will be rewarded with insight and understanding. Examine the scripture for yourselves. I would never have connected the wise and foolish virgins to the Book of Revelation if my companion had not enlightened me. However, let me guide you through this thoughtfully; let us raise some questions!

- Why has the bridegroom come?
- At what point is this taking place?
- Where are they going?

Matthew 25:10 tells us that they are going to a wedding feast.

'But while they were on their way to buy the oil, the bridegroom arrived. The virgins who were ready went in with him to the wedding banquet. And the door was shut' (Matt. 25:10).

Like the Galilean wedding, where the groom brings his bride and guests into his father's home, they arrive for the 'banquet'—the wedding feast. This signifies the second phase of the wedding, which the disciples would have known. Now, let us examine the verses of the 'Wise and Foolish Virgins' and explore how they relate to our prophetic journey.

Before this phase, the betrothal had already occurred—the acceptance of the cup from Jesus.

'At that time the kingdom of heaven will be like ten virgins who took their lamps and went out to meet the bridegroom' (Matt. 25:1).

These are not the same virgins as the brides; they are different ones who will illuminate the path just past midnight. These individuals represent the tribulation saints! They have been preparing themselves to join the wedding celebration. The bridegroom and the bride are mentioned in the Vulgate and Syriac versions. So, we read it as:

'At that time the kingdom of heaven will be like ten virgins who took their lamps and went out to meet the bridegroom ***'with His Bride'*** (Matt. 25:1) (Syriac).[12]

The New Testament was translated into Syriac as early as the second century, and by the fifth century, the entire Bible had been translated. So, who are the wise and foolish virgins?

Five were foolish, and five were wise. The foolish ones took their lamps but did not take any oil with them.

The wise ones, however, took oil in jars along with their lamps (Matt. 25:2–4)

Jesus employs familiar cultural references that the Galilean disciples could easily relate to, and the mentions of lamps and oil would likely have resonated with them.

Onwards.

The phrase 'at that time' in Matthew 24 explicitly links this event to the period before the King's return to Earth; it marks the moment when Jesus arrives, but it is not His second coming. This chapter highlights the indicators of the 'End of the Age,' the 'coming of the Son of Man,' and the 'lesson of the Fig Tree.' Importantly, it ends with the phrase, 'No one knows the Day nor the Hour,' linked to a Galilean wedding.

Matthew chapter 24 explores themes related to the disciples' questions at the beginning. However, Jesus goes beyond merely answering these questions.

'As Jesus was sitting on the Mount of Olives, the disciples came to him privately. "Tell us," they said, "when will this happen, and what will be the sign of your coming and of the end of the age?"'(Matt. 24:3).

He also discusses 'as in the days of Noah.' Chapter 24, near the end, will help us place 'The Wise and Foolish Virgins' within the context of prophecy. Jesus has already come to collect His bride. He compares the Kingdom of Heaven at that time to ten virgins who took their lamps and went to meet the bridegroom. Five were wise and had oil for their lamps; the others did not. While waiting, they all fell asleep. If you reflect on all the instances when Jesus used the phrase, 'The Kingdom of Heaven can be likened to,' you will notice that while here on Earth, those who believe in Christ will be among those who do not, within the Church.

'The bridegroom was a long time in coming, and they all became drowsy and fell asleep' (Matt. 24:3).

They fell asleep.

At midnight the cry rang out: 'Here's the bridegroom! Come out to meet him!' Then all the virgins woke up and trimmed their lamps. The foolish ones said to the wise, 'Give us some of your oil; our lamps are going out' (Matt. 25:6–8).

Would you kindly share some of your oil with us? This illustrates the blindness of these foolish individuals; they still fail to see the light. If the Holy Spirit dwells in you, the oil is within. They envy the wise ones for what they have. Remember, the Holy Spirit cannot be bought.

'"No," they replied, "there may not be enough for us and you. Instead, go to those who sell oil and buy some for yourselves"' (Matt. 25:9).

They did not realise that this oil could not be purchased. They claimed to know Christ, but an inner conversion never occurred. The Holy Spirit was never allowed to take root in their inner selves; yet they were religious. This is not sufficient: profession does not equal conversion!

'But while they were going to buy the oil, the bridegroom arrived. The virgins who were ready went in with him to the wedding banquet. And the door was shut' (Matt. 25:10).

The Syriac and Vulgate translations suggest he came with his bride. This aligns seamlessly with the prophetic imagery. The Lord Jesus will return with His bride (the Church) and gather those who have embraced Christ during the Great Tribulation on Earth (1 Thessalonians 3:13). They are on their way to the wedding feast.

We see there are several stages to Christ's coming; in 1 Thessalonians 3, we see:

'May he strengthen your hearts so that you will be blameless and holy in the presence of our God and Father when our Lord Jesus comes with all his holy ones*'* (1 Thess. 3:13).

He arrives with His 'holy ones' to gather the faithful remnant of tribulation saints who will accompany Him to the marriage feast; these are the wise virgins. The wise virgins accompanied him to the wedding feast, and the door was closed. It was too late for anyone else to enter the kingdom. When the other virgins arrived seeking admission, the bridegroom denied knowing them—a clear indication that they had never been born again.

'Later the others also came. "Lord," they said, "open the door for us!" But he replied, "Truly I tell you; I don't know you"' (Matt. 25:11–12).

This phrase echoes the phrase in Matthew 7:21–22 that says, *'Not everyone who says to me, "Lord, Lord," will enter the kingdom of heaven, but only the one who does the will of my Father who is in heaven.'*

Before we proceed to the next verse Jesus says, 'Only those who do the will of the Father.' The Gospel of John tells us His will!

'For my Father's will is that everyone who looks to the Son and believes in him shall have eternal life, and I will raise them up at the last day' (John 6:40).

Focusing on Christ and embracing His Spirit can assure us that His duty under the New Covenant is to save us. However, Jesus then says, 'Keep Watch.'

'Therefore keep watch, because you do not know the day or the hour' (Matt. 25:13).

By studying the Word of God, particularly the prophecies in Daniel 9, Revelation 6–19, and in the

Gospels, those living during the Great Tribulation can discern the timing of Jesus' second coming. I have mentioned this before. Those who live during the Great Tribulation and seek Jesus can identify the day, if not the hour. The books of Daniel and Revelation are often studied together because their prophecies about the end times align.

Both texts refer to different durations during the tribulation: Daniel mentions 1,290 days and 1,335 days, whereas Revelation cites 1,260 days. The 1,335 days referenced in Daniel signify the period from Jesus' arrival and encompass the judgement imposed on the world. Those who survive and are faithful to the Lord must endure until this timeframe is complete. This judgement distinguishes the sheep from the goats but differs from the Church's judgement. Now, let us continue.

Daniel 12:11–12: 'From the time that the daily sacrifice is abolished and the abomination that causes desolation is set up, there will be 1,290 days. Blessed is the one who waits for and reaches the end of the 1,335 days.'

The day that causes desolation? It is the same day that Jesus quotes in Matthew 24:15.

'"So when you see standing in the holy place 'the abomination that causes desolation,' spoken of through the prophet Daniel—let the reader understand—then

let those who are in Judea flee to the mountains' (Matt. 24:15–16).

Jesus speaks directly to the Jewish remnant, not to Christians, advising them to escape Judea. In this instance, He gives the Jews a hint about the right time to leave Jerusalem and to wait for 1,335 days. Why would He do this if He claims, 'No one knows the day or the hour'?

Something in a 'sacred place' in Jerusalem will be erected that is unholy. It may occur within a reconstructed temple or feature an idol in the 'Holy of Holies.' In Israel, the Temple Institute is actively searching for its Messiah and aims to build a new temple. To this end, they have gathered all essential equipment, personnel, protocols and strategies to restart animal sacrifices. This process could proceed swiftly thanks to modern technology, resources and knowledge.

Nevertheless, those living during that time, well acquainted with Daniel and the Book of Revelation, must flee. Jesus advises them, through His words, to await their redemption after 1,335 days. While we cannot foresee it now, they will know because Jesus instructs them to escape. God's wrath will be unleashed upon the world when the idol is set up in a holy place in Jerusalem or a reconstructed temple. Daniel references 1,290 days and John references 1,260 days, suggesting it takes an additional thirty days to halt the daily sacrifices and install the idol.

Daniel 9:27 gives us a clue:

He will confirm a covenant with many for one 'seven.' In the middle of the 'seven', he will end sacrifice and offering. And at the temple, he will set up an abomination that causes desolation, until the end that is decreed is poured out on him.

Now, let us silence the critics! Some argue that this desolation was fulfilled in AD 167 when Antiochus IV Epiphanes, the king of Syria, captured Jerusalem and desecrated the temple by offering a pig as a sacrifice on an altar to Zeus.

However, this is not the abomination Gabriel related to Daniel; Jesus quotes Daniel in Matthew 24:15 and Mark 13:14. He knew that this earlier desecration of the temple had already occurred, indicating that Daniel's prophecy remains significant for the future.

It is also asserted that when the Romans demolished the temple in AD 70, they sacrificed pigs; this act constituted the desolation. Regardless of this event, the Romans did not establish a covenant with the Jews, as indicated in that same verse, and no individual was appointed for worship; they merely destroyed the temple. During this era, the Romans harboured profound disdain for the Jews and pursued their annihilation. This abomination remains unfulfilled.

We veered off track for a moment. Let us return to our main topic. We focus on 'the day and hour of Jesus' coming' and 'like a thief in the night.' So, why does Jesus say we do not know the day or the hour? He refers to the Church, *not His* second coming. In a flash, in the twinkling of an eye, people will vanish, leaving only a lukewarm 'church' filled with unbelievers on the Earth.

During the tribulation period, it is possible to discern the 'day' concerning the timing of the second coming. It is imperative to avoid being left behind, but knowledge of His Word will provide a second chance. God ensures the presence of preachers in the world. Following the Church's departure from the Earth, supernatural preachers emerge as detailed in Revelation 6–19. Once a seven-year peace treaty is established and an idol is set up in a holy place, labelled the abomination of desolation, count 1,260 days and maintain vigilance.

Revelation 11:3 says, *'And I will appoint my two witnesses, and they will prophesy for 1,260 days, clothed in sackcloth.'*

These prophecies relate to specific periods associated with the seven-year tribulation and the 1,260 days. Jesus has gathered His bride during the Church's rapture and is on His way to the wedding feast. He pauses to collect a remnant known as the wise virgins. The bride has been in Heaven, preparing for the wedding feast while adorning herself in fine white linen. These wise and foolish virgins can be linked to the final church in Revelation. If the bride has been claimed, these virgins are experiencing the Great Tribulation—seven years of divine wrath on Earth. Jesus frequently references the Kingdom of Heaven, which includes wheat and weeds, representing the wise and the foolish.

My companion asked another question: Why are there ten virgins? This number seems odd, or does it? The number ten represents divine order and completion. Nothing in Jesus' Word is without purpose. When He returns for these guests, the end of this age approaches completion. He then splits the group into two fives. What does this signify? In biblical terms, the number five represents grace. Some will remain on Earth at the rapture, and individuals will come to faith in Him throughout the tribulation. This use of five symbolises God's 'Grace upon Grace' (five and five) for those who turn to Him during the Great Tribulation, while ten indicates the fulfilment of God's plan for the conclusion of this age. What an incredible Father we have, and what a blessing is His Son! Some have argued that these wise and foolish virgins are somehow connected to the Church of Christ. They are mistaken!

Chapter Nineteen - The Churches of Revelation 2 and 3

I once believed that the prophetic nature of the Book of Revelation was confined to chapters six and later. It never occurred to me that the entire book could be prophetic. I thought the churches referenced in chapters 2 and 3 merely represented churches from John's time! Scholars propose that chapters 2 and 3 fulfil two roles: they reference churches in John's time and prophesy about the Church throughout history. I found it challenging to embrace this concept. Nevertheless, I am now convinced that Revelations 2 and 3 foretell the state of the Church both in John's time and throughout history, including the period of the Great Tribulation.

In Chapters 2 and 3, Jesus Christ addresses the seven churches outlined in Revelation. Chapter 2 highlights four churches, starting with Ephesus, then Smyrna, followed by Pergamum (or Pergamos), and concluding with Thyatira, located southeast of Pergamum. In Chapter 3, He speaks to the last three churches: Sardis, Philadelphia and Laodicea, completing the discussion of all seven churches.

In chapter 1, He is portrayed standing amidst the seven lampstands, representing the seven churches—a spiritual reflection of His unwavering love for His Bride. He delivers His messages to John while simultaneously addressing the 'Angel of the Churches.' He remains the heart of the Church, overseeing her as a bride.

I believe the messages are not solely meant for the elders or church leaders of John's era; they hold significance beyond that because these leaders eventually pass away. Additionally, these messages are delivered to angels, who remain eternal and consistently support the churches throughout history. These divine messengers are entrusted to care for the churches. Our companions!

Jesus' general approach when addressing the churches in Revelation is first to highlight their strengths and weaknesses, then explain how to remedy these shortcomings. Finally, He warns them about ignoring the guidance of the Holy Spirit. Beyond physical churches, these letters address every member, particularly those with 'spiritual ears.' It concludes, 'Those who have ears, let them hear what the Spirit is saying.' The voice of the Spirit represents an eternal calling.

The letters sent to the churches, along with their comments, reach beyond the 'Seven Churches' to include all churches throughout history. In chapter 2, Smyrna's church stands out as one of the few that receives no condemnation, while the church in Thyatira is praised at first but later encounters harsh criticism. Various churches demonstrate different levels of obedience; some flourish in the face of persecution, while others yield to wealth and power.

There are seven types of churches. Today, churches encounter the same challenges that early congregations faced. Jesus guides the Church on how to tackle its problems. During Paul's missionary journeys, God initially barred him from preaching in the regions where the churches discussed in Revelation 2 and 3 are situated. Paul's team was '*kept by the Holy Spirit from preaching the word in the province of Asia*' (Acts 16:6)—Ephesus and its surrounding cities—but he eventually reached them on his third missionary journey.

We will not discuss the entirety of Revelation chapters 2 and 3; instead, we will focus on a specific phrase and integrate it into the prophetic timeline outlining the end of the age. There are seven churches, and the number seven symbolises perfection! The Apostles planted more than seven churches, yet Jesus only addresses seven! These two chapters deliver messages to all churches throughout history, including the present. In simple terms, Jesus informs each church of its strengths, weaknesses and areas for improvement. They represent various types of congregations.

Some try to categorise each church within a distinct historical period. For example, it is proposed that the first church, Ephesus, reflects the church's state from John's time until AD 100, with the following church covering AD 100 to approximately AD 300, and so forth. Although I find this perspective somewhat weak, the last two churches, Philadelphia and Laodicea, the sixth and seventh, represent the final days leading up to and during the Great Tribulation.

This distinction arises from a unique phrase that Jesus shares with the church of Philadelphia, which he does not extend to the other churches. Let us analyse this phrase. Jesus begins by commending the Philadelphians, noting their limited strength. They are among the few churches that receive favourable remarks from Him.

Let us go to Revelation Chapter 3, 'The Message to the Church at Philadelphia.' This is what He says is good about them. They have a little strength and the open door is an invitation to come inside (verse 8), but He then says in verse 10:

'Because you have kept My command to persevere, I also will keep you from ***the hour of trial*** *which shall come upon the whole world, to test those who dwell on the earth'* (Rev. 3:10).

This 'Hour of Trial' denotes the brief period within the seven years of tribulation described to John in the following chapters. This is the only church in which this is mentioned, but why? Because it is the sixth and penultimate church. He does not address this to the next one, Laodicea, the seventh and final church, which He criticises for being lukewarm (verse 17).

'Because you say, "I am rich, have become wealthy, and have need of nothing"—and do not know that you are wretched, miserable, poor, blind, and naked' (Rev. 3:17).

He then says in verse 20:

'Behold, I stand at the door and knock. If anyone hears My voice and opens the door, I will come in to him and dine with him, and he with Me' (Rev. 3:20).

He summons this assembly, and the Holy Spirit urges them to listen to His voice. At this moment, He speaks to both the wise and the foolish.

Today's church reflects the one in Philadelphia. Some of us hold dear our love for the Lord and honour His name, even if we sometimes feel we lack the strength of past generations; we are doing our best to persevere. We face challenges from various directions, but we stand together. Many Christians endure persecution and suffering for their beliefs, demonstrating remarkable resilience. Furthermore, although devoted teachers of the Word are few, their impact resonates deeply. Next, let us briefly pause to set the stage for what follows. We will look back at the parable of the 'Wise and Foolish Virgins'.

Jesus gathers His bride before joining the wedding feast, as explained in the chapter on 'The Galilean Wedding.' Let us see Jesus' 'Shofar.'

For the Lord Himself will descend from heaven with a shout, with the voice of an archangel, and with the trumpet of God. And the dead in Christ will rise first. Then we who are alive and remain shall be caught up together ***with them in the clouds to meet the Lord in the air.*** *And thus, we shall always be with the Lord* (1 Thess. 4:16–17).

This is the 'Flight of the Bride.'

Some believe this represents the seventh and last trumpet of Revelation 11:15 in the seven-trumpet sequence, heralding further tribulations on Earth. Specifically, the seventh trumpet apparently indicates the Church's presence during the Great Tribulation. However, this perspective is misguided.

In 1 Thessalonians 4:15, 'The Lord Himself will descend,' which signifies the trumpet of God. This trumpet differs from those mentioned in Revelation 8; it symbolises the trumpet call of the Bridegroom! Let us visit Revelation 8:

'When he opened the seventh seal, there was silence in heaven for about half an hour' (Rev. 8:1).

I am constantly drawn to 'Silence in Heaven,' which portrays the tense moment when witnesses encounter the emerging horrors. Heaven, I imagine, is anything but a silent place!

'And I saw the seven angels who stand before God, and seven trumpets were given to them' (Rev. 8:2).

Angels blow these trumpets!

Back to 1 Thessalonians 4:16:

'For the Lord Himself will descend from heaven with a shout, with the voice of an archangel, and with the trumpet of God. And the dead in Christ will rise first' (1 Thess. 4:16).

The Lord Jesus personally descends and blows this 'shofar' for His Bride. This is the trumpet call from Jesus; only the Bridegroom has the authority to sound His trumpet. This trumpet is not given to any angel. The voice of an archangel embodies the strength and authority of this sound.

In Matthew, when Jesus speaks about the wise and foolish virgins, He gathers those who turn to Christ during the great tribulation that is to come upon the earth. These are the wise ones filled with the oil of the Holy Spirit. When Jesus comes with His Bride, He takes these believers from the world into Heaven. Those left on Earth believed they were filled with the Spirit but were lukewarm and foolish. Jesus says to the Laodiceans!

'I know your deeds, that you are neither cold nor hot. I wish you were either one or the other. So, because you are lukewarm—neither hot nor cold—I am about to spit you out of my mouth' (Rev. 3:15–16).

This accusation targets the so-called church of Laodicea. When Jesus' followers leave the earth, Laodicea's congregation continues to endure the Great Tribulation. These are the individuals whom Jesus accuses, saying, 'I never knew you,' as recorded in Matthew 7:21–23. The context is that Jesus speaks about the fruits of people's lives. However, individuals will also be saved as the truth becomes clear. Inner conversion had never occurred before this.

Let us take a moment to summarise, as this topic has many layers, and it is crucial to understand the insights being shared. In our current age, I believe we are in the unique position of being the penultimate church, known as Philadelphia. Jesus comes to collect His Bride. We cannot tell when this will happen, but it will occur in the twinkling of an eye.

Upon departing from Earth, we ascend to Heaven to prepare for the wedding feast, adorning ourselves in 'fine white linen' (Revelation 19:8). However, there will be those left behind who believed they were acceptable. Let us remind ourselves that a profession of faith that does not result in genuine inner conversion is insufficient. The church left on Earth is the Laodicean 'church,' filled with lukewarm people.

After getting ready for the wedding feast, Jesus gathers the 'wise' from the Great Tribulation on His way to the banquet, and together we head to the Father's house for the celebration. The doors are firmly locked, sparking questions from those left behind on Earth, who are labelled the 'foolish'. What an adventure. Nevertheless, there is still more!

Chapter Twenty - Jesus and the Fig Tree

We need to examine how Jesus embodied righteousness and steadfastly fulfilled God's will. Let us establish a prophetic foundation by considering the last six months of His life, beginning with the Feast of Tabernacles, the last celebration of the Hebrew calendar. This event took place approximately six months prior to the next Passover, which heralded a new year and His crucifixion.

A conversation between Jesus and the Holy Spirit is recorded in Luke 13:6–9*;* however, let us provide some context. In the earlier chapters, Jesus condemned the Pharisees for their outward cleanliness while ignoring their inner flaws. He called on the audience to prepare themselves, repent and keep their lamps lit. Chapter 13 opens with a tragic development—a massacre has taken place.

The Governor of Judea commanded the execution of those making sacrifices. Information about this event is limited. It is believed that the victims were Galileans. Many thought that their deaths were a punishment for grievous sins, which Jesus later compares with other incidents. Jesus opposes the authorities, and everyone is listening.

'And Jesus answered and said to them, "Do you suppose that these Galileans were worse sinners than all other Galileans because they suffered such things?"' (Luke 13:2)

In verse 6, a conversation unfolds between a man with a fig tree and his gardener. The man symbolises Jesus, the gardener represents the Holy Spirit, and the fig tree denotes Israel, all within a vineyard that signifies the world. Let us explore this insightful part of the chapter.

'Then he told this parable: "A man ***[Jesus]*** *had a fig tree* ***[Israel]*** *growing in his vineyard* ***[World]****, and he went to look for fruit on it but did not find any."'*

Remember that Jesus used parables to illustrate spiritual truths through earthly examples. He came to His people, Israel, who witnessed miraculous signs and wondrous acts. Jesus taught them about righteous living but found no fruit. Their leaders oppressed and controlled the people. Recall that He had recently accused the Pharisees of not being clean on the inside. The Pharisees were listening.

So he said to the man who took care of the vineyard ***[The Holy Spirit]****, "For three years now, I* ***[Jesus]*** *have been coming to look for fruit on this fig tree* ***[Israel]*** *and have not found any. Cut it down! Why should it use up the soil?* (Luke 13:7)

For three years, I have committed myself to serving the people. They are spiritually blind and yearn only for signs and wonders. The Lord Jesus says, 'Cut down the fig tree,' it is unproductive, it yields nothing. As noted in Luke 3:23, Jesus commenced His ministry at thirty and is now thirty-three.

'"Sir," the man ***[The Holy Spirit]*** *replied, "leave it alone for one more year, and I will dig around it and fertilise it"'* (Luke 13:8).

The Holy Spirit addresses Jesus as 'Sir.' What humility! Amazingly, God would refer to God as 'Sir.' The respect and humility in this touched my heart—the Holy Spirit advocates for Israel.

'"If it bears fruit next year, fine! If not, then cut it down"' (Luke 13:9).

The gardener requests additional time. 'Wait another year. Give it a chance,' he urges. 'I will continue to care for it.' Six months later, during the next Passover, they crucified our Lord. However, the Holy Spirit sought time; He specifically requested a year. The final attempt came later when the Holy Spirit made one last appeal through Stephen in Acts chapter 7, where he details the history of Israel from Abraham to that era. Although there is no conclusive evidence regarding the timing of Stephen's martyrdom, the Holy Spirit did request a year.

Why? To remind them of their national heritage and inspire feelings of regret for distancing themselves from the Messiah. I feel tearful each time I read about Stephen in this narrative. The grace of God shown here is extraordinarily remarkable. The name Stephen represents a garland or crown and holds deep spiritual significance. The Holy Spirit offers them one last chance. Stephen defended Christ, encouraging them to remember their roots and heritage. Despite the Pharisees' opposition, they could not resist him, which led to him being brought before the High Priest to answer charges (Acts 7:1–2).

Then the high priest asked Stephen, "Are these charges true?" He replied: "Brothers and fathers, listen to me! The God of glory appeared to our father Abraham while he was still in Mesopotamia, before he lived in Harran" (Acts 7:2).

The Holy Spirit begins to outline their history through Stephen. Until the judgements in verses 51–52, he has nothing positive to convey about them before they stoned him.

'"You stiff-necked people! Your hearts and ears are still uncircumcised. You are just like your ancestors: You always resist the Holy Spirit!' (Acts 7:51)

Then the judgement: God sends messengers, prophets and His own Son!

Was there ever a prophet your ancestors did not persecute? They even killed those who predicted the coming of the Righteous One. And now you have betrayed and murdered him—you who have received the law that was given through angels but have not obeyed it" (Acts 7:52–53).

They proceed to stone Stephen to death for the truth that stung their souls. **The time is up**! The fig tree will now be cut down. Eventually, the temple will be destroyed, and they will be driven out of the land. The Jews are now judged for crucifying Jesus and ultimately killing Stephen. The Holy Spirit made one final attempt, even after Jesus was crucified. This reflects the grace of our God, who is full of divine mercy, even in the face of hatred. God has turned His back on Israel and will establish the Church, founded on Christ as the cornerstone and His messengers, the Apostles. Following the 'times of the Gentiles,' He will return to save Israel. All Israel will be redeemed at His revelation when they look upon the one they have pierced.

Chapter Twenty-one - Covert Entry

Continuing the detour. Six months before His death, Jesus hesitated to travel to Jerusalem because of plots against Him. Still, He entered the city quietly during the Feast of Tabernacles. It was not yet His time to die; that event would occur at the next Passover. As His opponents searched for Him, animosity towards Jesus grew stronger. The Feast of Tabernacles is one of the key events in the Jewish calendar. It occurs during harvest time and celebrates the Jews' period of living in temporary shelters or booths (tents) after leaving Egypt. It is the last of the seven feasts.

This season is marked by joy as it anticipates the day when the Messiah will reign, allowing the Jewish nation to dwell in the land in peace and prosperity. The first three days of this feast passed without anyone seeing Jesus (John 7:14). The crowds wondered whether He would come and claim to be the Messiah. Then, halfway through the feast, He began teaching in the temple courts. The religious authorities assumed that a person had either studied in a traditional school or was self-taught. However, Jesus' response revealed a third option: His teaching was from God, who had sent Him.

The Feast of Tabernacles included various festival rituals, one of which commemorated the water that flowed from the rock during the wilderness journey. The seventh and final day of the feast featured a significant celebration before God (Leviticus 23:36). This establishes the context: it is the feast's concluding day, serving as the closing ceremony of John 7.

As the festival concludes, a magnificent celebration unfolds to mark the completion of the year's final Torah reading. The Torah consists of the first five books of the Hebrew Bible: Genesis, Exodus, Leviticus, Numbers and Deuteronomy.

On the last and greatest day of the festival, Jesus stood and said in a ***loud voice****, 'Let anyone who is thirsty come to me and drink. Whoever believes in me, as Scripture has said, rivers of living water will flow from within them'* (John 7:37–38).

This occurred during the Feast of Tabernacles. Jesus stood up and shouted in the temple; typically, priests and the people remained seated and silent, but Jesus stood and cried out. This would have infuriated them, as he was not supposed to behave this way. This feast is one that all Jewish men aged twelve or older celebrate in Jerusalem. By age fifty, they have visited Jerusalem numerous times, making them well-versed in the proceedings.

Ceremonies occur daily during the feast, honouring the blessings of the year and the fall of the barrier between God and Israel. This is the final day of the feast. For this event, the priests are divided into groups to perform various tasks, each assigned to prepare for the grand ceremony.

The first group, primarily priests, would remain at the temple, preparing for the rituals, waiting for a sign to begin and praising God once the other two groups had finished their duties.

The second group journeyed to the Kidron Valley, where they gathered willow branches to symbolise resurrection. They waved these branches over the altar of sacrifice, imitating the sound of rushing wind to commemorate the day God ignited the altar of Solomon's temple. They patiently awaited the signal at the eastern gate.

The final group followed the High Priest to the Siloam pool, where he filled a silver pitcher with water while singing Isaiah 12. I will quote just the first three verses.

In that day you will say: "I will praise you, LORD. Although you were angry with me, your anger has turned away and you have comforted me. Surely God is my salvation; I will trust and not be afraid. The LORD, the LORD himself, is my strength and my defense; he has become my salvation." With joy you will draw water from the wells of salvation (Isa. 12:1–3).

This Messianic Prophecy expresses the concept of salvation by drawing water from a well. Once completed and after waiting at the gates, all the groups settled in, and the gathering fell silent as everyone awaited the ceremony's commencement, a tradition lasting 1,500 years. Various tales describe how the proceedings begin. Typically, there is complete silence in eager anticipation of a signal. However, Jesus stands up and calls out loudly!

'On the last and greatest day of the festival, Jesus stood and said in a loud voice, "Let anyone who is thirsty come to me and drink. Whoever believes in me, as Scripture has said, rivers of living water will flow from within them"' (John 7:37–38).

The Living Water flows through Jesus; this is the Holy Spirit.

'By this he meant the Spirit, whom those who believed in him were later to receive. Up to that time the Spirit had not been given, since Jesus had not yet been glorified' (John 7:39).

This was not cricket! They were waiting for the signal. Jesus standing up and interrupting the ceremony would have infuriated the Pharisees. All this occurs on the last day of the feast, and the next day, they have a small closing celebration. This is when they confronted Jesus with the woman caught in adultery. This last minor feast was meant to be a day of great rejoicing among the ordinary Jews, but instead of leading the celebrations, the leaders confronted Jesus. They were furious.

Chapter Twenty-Two – The Woman Caught in Adultery

Following the feast, the leaders are enraged by Jesus and try to trap Him. The next day, after coming down from the Mount of Olives, Jesus teaches in the temple. While He is speaking, a group of Scribes and Pharisees interrupts, bringing a woman and claiming she committed adultery and was caught in the act.

The teachers of the law and the Pharisees brought in a woman caught in adultery. They made her stand before the group and said to Jesus, "Teacher, this woman was caught in the act of adultery. In the Law, Moses commanded us to stone such women. Now what do you say?" They were using this question as a trap, to have a basis for accusing him. ***But Jesus bent down*** *and started to write on the ground with his finger (John 8:3–6).*

They were looking to trick Jesus. They had already judged this woman.

When they kept questioning him, he straightened up and said to them, "Let any one of you who is without sin be the first to throw a stone at her." Again, he stooped down and wrote on the ground. At this, those who heard began to go away one at a time, the older ones first, until only Jesus was left, with the woman still standing there (John 8:7–9).

When an individual is found guilty of adultery, a specific process must be followed. Sotah, a term used in Talmudic literature for a woman suspected of infidelity, refers to her undergoing a trial to prove her guilt or innocence. In Numbers 5:11–31, the ritual that a priest carries out in the Tabernacle is outlined to ascertain whether a woman, whom her husband believes has committed adultery, is indeed guilty.

*'Then he shall take some **holy water** in a clay jar and put some dust from the tabernacle floor into the water'* (Num. 5:17).

In cases of adultery, both the man and woman, along with witnesses, were required to be present. However, the religious leaders brought only the woman to Jesus, excluding any witnesses or the man, which contradicted the Law. At this moment, Jesus was in the temple courts, not the Tabernacle, where this accusation should have occurred. It is crucial to note that He was the one who delivered the Law to the Jews.

Jesus kneels in reverence to God, seeking guidance from the Holy Spirit. He writes in the dust with a finger—the same finger that engraved the Ten Commandments in stone for Moses to share with the Israelites. I was curious about why God chose stone for the inscription of the Ten Commandments, but my companion pointed out that the heart is like stone, emphasising that only God can touch a person's heart to imprint His Laws upon it.

However, our Lord wrote in the dust. This dust symbolises mercy; the wind carries it away. Jesus demonstrates the correct approach by exposing their failure to follow the Law. Mixing dust with holy water is unnecessary since through Jesus comes the living water. Then Jesus stood up and proclaimed, '*Let anyone without sin throw the first stone*!' Can you imagine Jesus picking up a stone and offering it to the Pharisees? These Pharisees would remember Jeremiah.

'LORD, you are the hope of Israel; ***all who forsake you will be put to shame. Those who turn away from you will be written in the dust because they have forsaken the LORD, the spring of living water'*** (Jer. 17:13).

Jesus' writing in the dust recalls Jeremiah, a figure familiar to the people since they began reading the Torah at age twelve in a yearly cycle. Their behaviour mirrored Jeremiah's prophecy: those who stray are recorded in the dust, having forsaken their Messiah.

Through Him comes the 'Living Water of the Spirit.' The priests, scribes and Pharisees were aware of their actions. The scribes, a group dedicated to copying and teaching the Scriptures, and the Pharisees sought to ensnare the Lord Jesus into making an incorrect statement so they could accuse Him. However, they failed. The older people turned away first, realising sooner than the younger ones.

'Jesus straightened up and asked her, "Woman, where are they? Has no one condemned you?" "No one, sir," she said. "Then neither do I condemn you," Jesus declared. "Go now and leave your life of sin" (John 8:10–11).

Jesus recognised her actions and said, 'Leave your life of sin.' Instead of judging her, He extended forgiveness. He applied the Law fairly, embodying mercy and granting pardon; ultimately, He would bear the penalty. Her name was written in the dust but disappeared when the wind blew.

The Torah is read in weekly sections corresponding with the Hebrew calendar, spanning up to fifty-five weeks, depending on the lunar cycle. This cycle concludes with the Jewish festival of Simchat Torah, the last day of the celebration. Everyone knew the law concerning immorality, yet it should be practised and enforced with absolute integrity. They aimed to trap Jesus into making statements that could be used against Him, but as the ultimate High Priest, He did exactly what was required. He not only taught the Law but also fulfilled it entirely.

Before we proceed, it is essential to note that some versions of the Bible include footnotes or enclose '*The Woman Caught in Adultery*' in brackets or italics, raising questions about its inclusion. This discrepancy arises from variations in the ancient texts used as the basis for their translation.

There is no question in my mind that this passage is exactly where it is meant to be. Some people think it should not be part of scripture at all, or that it should be placed elsewhere, as it contains words and phrases that John does not typically use. Some scholars even try to link it to Luke.

It is also said that church leaders do not welcome its inclusion because it somehow relegates the sin of adultery to a 'soft' sin and therefore sends the wrong message to church members.

As I understand it, all sins ultimately lead to judgment. Does it make a difference whether a sin is considered minor or major? I do not think so. In my opinion, if you break one point of God's Law, you break the whole law, and your ultimate destination is not determined by how grave the sin is. It is defined by your commitment to Christ and whether the Holy Spirit is truly in you. We ought not to sin, yet we do. Simply being a Christian does not equate to perfection. This is why Christ intercedes for us day and night in heaven.

Although this passage of scripture may not be present in the earliest manuscripts, its inclusion was not an error. I have confidence that God, through His Holy Spirit, was able to guide individuals during the formative period of the New Testament and in the final compilation of the Word of God to incorporate elements that may or may not have been present in the original texts. Consider what the writer articulates in the final chapter.

(John 21:24) This is the disciple who testifies to these things and who wrote them down. We know that his testimony is true.

(John 21:25) Jesus did many other things as well. If every one of them were written down, I suppose that even the whole world would not have room for the books that would be written.

Its inclusion does not change the message of salvation; instead, it underscores the grace of forgiveness in the work of Christ. Onwards.

Part One Summary

Before we move on to part two, let us reflect on our journey thus far. The United Kingdom holds unique significance in God's heart due to its ties to the Jewish remnant after the diaspora. God favoured this compact group of islands, transforming it into a mighty empire that spread the Good News wherever it established colonies. Unfortunately, our nation has drifted away from God.

After the last world war, many men and women arrived here from countries that had received the good news, bringing hope to help us rise from the brink. Reflecting on this, I cannot help but feel God's deep concern for His people in this country and its decline. Thankfully, He has generously extended His grace by reminding the Church of His love and mercy through these remarkable individuals who carry heartfelt messages from Heaven, encouraging us to return to Him. Interestingly, in places where Christianity is suppressed, the Church seems to flourish. Regrettably, we cannot say the same about our situation here.

The Bible encounters numerous challenges from both external sources and within the Church. Critics of the Bible seem to be gaining ground in this ongoing struggle. In our studies of the creation narrative, we found that it not only recounts the act of creation but also reveals God's redemptive plan. Meanwhile, the influence of evolution appears to be spreading.

Examining Scripture closely reveals that it resembles a meticulously woven tapestry, rich in complex patterns that unfold through sincere seeking and steadfast dedication to the Holy Spirit. God invites us to reconnect with Him.

Depending on perspective, we are both engaged and married to Him if we take the 'Cup.' The Last Supper establishes a New Covenant, signifying the commencement of our engagement when considered in context. As His bride and inheritance, He will return for us, as expressed in the 'Galilean Wedding.' Upon His ascension to Heaven, He did not forsake us; instead, He provided us with a helper to assist in our preparation for the wedding feast and safeguard us from peril.

There are two groups of people in the church: those who profess Christ as their saviour and those who have never fully accepted our Lord. The church consists of both the wise and the foolish. However, only the wise will be taken from the world when He returns for His followers. Even so, the foolish are given another chance during the 'Great Tribulation.'

The Book of Revelation continues to perplex many individuals, who either avoid it or regard it merely as 'spiritual warfare' and consider it irrelevant to our lives. Additionally, some interpret this book solely in an allegorical context, contending that it pertains exclusively to the Church due to God's purported rejection of Israel. In the following section, we will explain how inaccurate these interpretations are.

PART TWO

Chapter One – Completing Redemption

Throughout His life, our Lord embodied all righteousness. This narrative began with a discussion about the creation pattern, which we propose also represents an outline of redemption.

Jesus entered creation on the first day as a spiritual light for the world. On the fourth day, the stars illuminated the heavens and the earth. This also reflects a pattern for Jesus' physical coming into the world. The Passover Lamb first entered the homes of the Lord's people in Israel, with its blood safeguarding them from the judgement against their firstborn, but this was only for that specific occasion. On the fourth day, they offered this lamb as a sacrifice.

Jesus entered His home in Jerusalem, where He received a warm welcome. Just four days later, He was crucified as the Lamb of God. On the first day, He arrived, and by the fourth day, He was put to death. This sacrificial Lamb atoned for the sins of all humanity. Those who embrace Him find salvation from the impending judgement on the earth.

'But this Man, after He had offered one sacrifice for sins forever, sat down at the right hand of God' (Hebrews 10:12).

Is there a pattern apparent in a different context? The seven feasts of Israel, crucial to the Jewish agricultural calendar, are divided into Spring and Autumn celebrations. Jesus has fulfilled the first four Spring feasts and will return to accomplish the last three. This event will initiate the judgements in Revelation, restoring His authority over the earth and renewing creation. The last three days emphasise the redemption depicted in the creation narrative, where Jesus will eliminate the curse from the earth and usher in peace for all creation.

How does this connect to the seven days of creation? The first four days are complete, as noted earlier. It took seven days from the crucifixion to the resurrection; He was crucified on the fourth day and resurrected on the seventh. Through His sacrifice, He conquered the principalities and rulers of the heavenly realms, freeing the Old Testament saints from their holding place known as Abraham's Bosom. He holds the keys to death and Hades, symbolising spiritual victory.

This occurred after seven days, marking a victorious spiritual struggle; however, the world still groans under the burden of sin. Consequently, Christ must return in the autumn to complete the last three feasts on Earth, judge humanity and liberate creation. On the seventh and final day, the earth will find rest and be freed from the curse on creation, with Christ ruling for a thousand years in Jerusalem. A day equates to a thousand years, and a thousand years to a day (2 Peter 3:8). Ultimately, during the millennium, the earth will have rest from the consequences of sin's curse, when He returns to reign as King from Jerusalem and over the world as King of Kings and Lord of Lords (Revelation 17:14; 19:16). We will address this in more depth later.

Chapter Two – Why Should We Support Israel?

How can we integrate this question into the prophetic timeline? It is straightforward, as all prophecy focuses on Israel, whether directly or indirectly. The Redeemer, born a Jew, came to the Jewish people. Upon accepting Jesus, we are transformed into new creations; at that point, we are neither Jews nor Gentiles. For many, Israel presents a challenge. Hatred against Jews has been a persistent issue throughout history.

Demonstrations against Israel regarding the war in Gaza illustrate this point. What disturbs me is that people are misled, jumping on the bandwagon driven by social media. I heard a reporter questioning demonstrators who were waving banners with anti-Jewish messages during a pro-Palestinian rally. Many held signs that read, 'From the river to the sea, Palestine will be free,' prompting a reporter to ask, 'From which river to which sea?' Some suggested the Red Sea, while others mentioned the Baltic Sea, indicating they were misled and simply following the crowd. The river refers to the Jordan, and the sea is the

Mediterranean. This phrase partly originates from Psalm 72:8: *'from the river to the ends of the earth.'*

The era we live in reflects the past since Israel's inception. The Jewish people remain a mystery. Descending from the sons of Jacob through a promise, they have repeatedly faced efforts from individuals, nations and dark forces to annihilate them, yet they persist. Enduring animosity at every corner, they inhabit a small region comparable in size to Wales. Despite this, they constitute a strong, thriving and resource-rich nation embroiled in conflict since before 1948, which continues to endure.

It is intriguing to note that the Church, originally a Jewish institution in Judea, is now regarded as Israel's successor following the rejection of Christ. Jewish believers in their Messiah founded the Church and authored nearly all its key texts. Furthermore, the biblical prophecies concerning Israel's blessing and restoration to the Promised Land are frequently interpreted allegorically as assurances of God's favour for the Church.

Today, many Christians share a widely-held view with deep historical roots. The basis of these theologies, along with various perspectives contributing to antisemitism, can be traced back to the first days of Christianity and even earlier. I hope you recognise that prophecy necessitates the presence of Israel in the promised land for its fulfilment.

This discussion aims to trace prophecy from Genesis to Revelation. However, for many Christians, the Old Testament is seen as irrelevant since it is believed that the Church holds all the promises. As a result, it is often regarded as inapplicable, with elements interpreted as figurative language.

Convincing these individuals will be challenging because we have lost half of the Bible. However, the Apostle Paul of the New Testament also faced difficulties regarding people's perceptions of the Jews due to this 'New Way.' Additionally, his assertions that God has not rejected the Jews and has saved a remnant for Himself are often ignored.

From the onset, a deep animosity towards the Jews emerged, significantly influenced by certain prominent church Fathers. They placed the blame for Jesus' death on the Jews, overlooking the fact that Jesus was Jewish and sacrificed himself for everyone. Naming these church fathers is unnecessary, as the list is extensive; it suffices to reference the decrees of the Council of Nicaea.

The First Council of Nicaea occurred in AD 325. This significant Christian assembly was convened to resolve a dispute regarding Jesus' divinity and several other matters. Notably, the council decided to shift the observance of the Resurrection from the Jewish Feast of First Fruits to Easter, creating a separation from Jewish celebrations.

The Council of Nicaea (AD 325 in Turkey) stated: 'For it is unbecoming beyond measure that on this holiest of festivals, we should follow the customs of the Jews. Henceforth, let us have nothing in common with these odious people.'[13]

The Reformation did not lead to improvements. Although initially sympathetic, Martin Luther later wrote hateful things about them. So, are we surprised by the current antisemitism related to the Church? The Jewish people never had a chance, and these church fathers dismissed Paul of the New Testament and his assertions that God was not finished with the Jews.

The Book of Revelation includes the Church in its initial three chapters, but is absent until the final chapter. Nonetheless, this theology asserts that chapters 6–19 pertain to the Church. These sections are interpreted allegorically to align with their beliefs. Given the confusion surrounding Israel, its refusal to repent and being back in the land, we need to analyse God's complete guidance to determine whether Israel's return arises from human will or divine intention.

You see, three weeks after 7th October 2023, I was asked a question in a group forum by Christians who despised what they observed Israel doing to the Palestinians. It was termed genocide. In that short time, they had forgotten about the 7th October; since then, anger against Israel has intensified. On that forum, it was suggested that Israel's rebirth without repentance challenges the biblical fulfilment of prophecy because they are unrepentant and back in the land. Many scriptures indicate that when Israel repents, God will return them to the land. They are correct; they have not repented but are back in the land. Let us examine one of the scriptures quoted on the forum and in a message.

When all these blessings and curses I have set before you come on you and you take them to heart wherever the LORD your God disperses you among the nations, and when you and your children return to the LORD your God and obey him with all your heart and with all your soul according to everything, I command you today, then the LORD your God will restore your fortunes and have compassion on you and gather you again from all the nations where he scattered you. Even if you have been banished to the most distant land under the heavens, from there, the LORD your God will gather you and bring you back (Deut. 30:1–4).

Well, that looks terrible. They are liberal and morally conflicted in many ways, like the rest of the world, but also filled with hardline Jewish fundamentalists who are still awaiting the Messiah. However, we must compare scripture with scripture and understand that God knew Israel, as a nation, would never repent of its terrible ways. This is symptomatic of all humanity, condemned by its sinful nature, so it is to be expected.

If we examine prophecy concerning the land, they occupy only a tiny part of the original promise. This indicates the spiritual state of an unrepentant Israel. They have not moved into the promise in any way.

Today, like much of the world, a significant portion of Israel identifies as secular. This means they have no religious ties, hold liberal views, and include many hardliners, moderates and a rebellious Generation Z (and Generation Alpha may be just as challenging).

However, Israel is wealthy, powerful and capable of defending itself. Yes, she embodies the biblical notion of a harlot who did not repent before 1948, yet she is back in the land promised by God, and against all odds, she has never been defeated in war since 1948.

In 1948, Israel was established as a nation, and a small Jewish community faced significant challenges as war broke out. Surprisingly, they not only endured but also expanded their territory. The Arab-Israeli War of 1948 began shortly after Israel declared independence on 14 May, when five Arab countries launched an invasion.

They should not have triumphed in that war; while America expressed sympathy, it did not extend assistance. A closer look reveals numerous miracles suggesting divine intervention. Since then, Israel has faced multiple wars, and American support in the form of military aid only began in 1967. I believe this was driven by America's desire for allies in the Middle East, and our Lord, knowing the future, also had something to say about this.

Unrepentant Israel! What will bring them to repentance? It suffices to state that Jesus' appearance will motivate all of Israel to turn back, but this will not happen until the Spirit of the Lord is poured out on them, as Zechariah foretold.

'And I will pour out on the house of David and the inhabitants of Jerusalem a spirit of grace and supplication. They will look on me, the one they have pierced, and they will mourn for him as one mourns for an only child and grieve bitterly for him as one grieves for a firstborn son' (Zech. 12:10).

Repentance is the only path for the nation of Israel; however, this perspective pertains to the future and may not satisfy those who argue they should not reside in the land, notably some Christians. We will delve into the argument that repentance is irrelevant due to the Abrahamic Covenant. While many claim the New Testament has replaced the Old Testament, they frequently refer to the Old Testament for support when it aligns with their agendas.

Under the Mosaic Covenant, the curses and blessings bestowed upon Israel were always present. The destruction of the First Temple signifies God's displeasure with Israel, resulting in their removal from the land. Daniel and his people were taken to Babylon, where they served King Nebuchadnezzar. From this period, we receive the remarkable Book of Daniel, which provides a glimpse into Israel's future.

Daniel described the reconstruction of the Second Temple and the Messiah's coming. In Chapter Twelve, he outlines the impending judgement on Israel's future, which can only occur after the Messiah's death and Israel's return to the Land.

When Jesus arrived, the Second Temple had already been constructed; yet, He foretold its destruction. After Jesus' crucifixion and, I might add, Stephen's martyrdom, God expelled them from the land. Jesus established a New Covenant through His blood, encompassing all nations that come to Him with repentance. In contrast, the old Covenant, known as the Law of Moses, did not provide salvation and was given explicitly to the Jews. The purpose of the Law was to highlight sin.

'The sting of death is sin, and the power of sin is the law' (1 Cor. 15:56).

Everyone who comes to Christ is saved through the New Covenant, not just the Jews. The strength of this promise arises from our saviour's death! Nevertheless, Israel as a nation remains unrepentant and has returned to the land. Why, then, have they come back despite their lack of repentance? We should examine the Abrahamic Covenant, which was established before the Law was given, between God and Abraham. Let us reflect on the moment God first called Abraham, who was initially named Abram.

Until this time, Abram was a pagan worshipper, and his father, Terah, was a pagan priest. After the flood, God sought to establish a nation to demonstrate to the world that following His ways would bring blessings. First, He needed to grow a nation. As mentioned earlier, Israel is the only nation God purposely established in the world. Babylon, or 'Babel,' was the very first nation recorded in the Bible, seeded by a man called Nimrod. This was a demonic nation.

Let us go to Genesis 12:1–5:

The LORD had said to Abram, 'Go from your country, your people and your father's household to the land I will show you. I will make you into a great nation, and I will bless you; I will make your name great, and you will be a blessing.'

Abram was seventy-five years old when he first received God's promise, and Genesis 21:5 indicates that he was 100 at Isaac's birth; Sarai was ninety. It took twenty-five years for God to eventually fulfil His promise. In the interim, he attempts to aid God in addressing his dilemma of being old and unable to accept a life without children with Sarai (Sarah), his wife. In Hebrew, Sarai means 'my princess.' Ultimately, God will change both of their names.

'I will bless those who bless you, and whoever curses you I will curse; and all peoples on earth will be blessed through you.' So Abram went, as the LORD had told him; and Lot went with him. Abram was seventy-five years old when he set out from Harran. He took his wife Sarai, his nephew Lot, all the possessions they had accumulated and the people they had acquired in Harran, and they set out for the land of Canaan, and they arrived there (Gen. 12:3–5).

God called Abram and vowed to establish a nation through him. He guarantees that anyone who blesses Abram will also be blessed, while those who curse him will face a curse in return. At this point, however, there is no promise of land; the blessing pertains only to his descendants, although God will eventually reveal the land to him. God made a covenant with Abram, referred to as the Abrahamic Covenant. Moving ahead to Genesis 15, Abram is confused. While God vowed to create nations through him, he had no descendants, and his wife, Sarai, was unable to bear children. Let us look at the first five verses.

After this, the word of the LORD came to Abram in a vision: 'Do not be afraid, Abram. I am your shield, your very great reward.' But Abram said, 'Sovereign LORD, what can you give me since I remain childless and the one who will inherit my estate is Eliezer of Damascus?' (Gen. 15:1–2)

He has no son and believes the promise may be fulfilled through a relative. However, God has other ideas, Abram retorts!

And Abram said, 'You have given me no children; so a servant in my household will be my heir.' Then the word of the LORD came to him: 'This man will not be your heir, but a son who is your own flesh and blood will be your heir.' He took him outside and said, 'Look up at the sky and count the stars—if indeed you can count them.' Then he said to him, 'So shall your offspring be.' (Gen. 15:3–5)

God is going to give him a son.

'Abram believed the LORD, and he credited it to him as righteousness' (Gen. 15:6).

Abram's trust prompted Him to establish a covenant. This agreement, known as the Abrahamic Covenant, remains relevant today, unlike the Mosaic Covenant and its associated curses, which were fulfilled and replaced by the New Covenant upon Christ's death for those who believe in Him.

Now, let us examine this covenant verse by verse.

'He also said to him, *"I am the LORD, who brought you out of Ur of the Chaldeans to give you this land to take possession of it." But Abram said, "Sovereign LORD, how can I know that I will gain possession of it?"* (Gen. 15:7–8)

Abram starts to doubt when he asks God, 'How can I be sure?'

'So the LORD said to him, "Bring me a heifer, a goat and a ram, each three years old, along with a dove and a young pigeon"' (Gen. 15:9).

This covenant, which required blood, was established before the Law of Moses was introduced. God is now prepared to confirm this covenant with an oath between them. Why these animals? The Book of Leviticus describes the animal offerings.

- Heifer is a priestly offering
- Goat is a sin offering
- Ram is a substitutionary offering
- Dove and pigeon consecrated Abraham's firstborn son (Isaac) as Jesus in Luke 2:24

When the time came for the purification rites required by the Law of Moses, Joseph and Mary took him to Jerusalem to present him to the Lord (as it is written in the Law of the Lord, 'Every firstborn male is to be consecrated to the Lord'), and to offer a sacrifice in keeping with what is said in the Law of the Lord: ***'a pair of doves or two young pigeons'*** *(Luke 2:22–24).*

Abram carried out the Lord's instructions.

Abram brought all these to Him, cut them in two and arranged the halves opposite each other; the birds, however, he did not cut in half. Then birds of prey came down on the carcasses, but Abram drove them away (Gen. 15:10–11).

Abram needs to bring three animals, cut each in half, and arrange the halves in a line opposite each other. This setup will cause their blood to flow onto the ground, creating a flood between the separated parts.

Recognising the culture surrounding oath-taking in Abram's era is essential to grasping the purpose here. Keep in mind the context, culture and audience! In ancient times, particularly in the East, taking an oath was a serious event. Animals were split in two, forming a pool of blood on the ground between the divided carcasses. Oaths would be taken and both parties would walk between the pieces to seal the oaths, with blood mingling on their bare feet. Anyone who broke the oath would deserve to end up like the dead animals on the ground. They all passed between the pieces of the animal carcasses, walking through the blood.

'Abram brought all these to him, cut them in two and arranged the halves opposite each other; the birds, however, he did not cut in half' (Gen. 15:10).

These birds of prey, in the next verse, were likely included in scripture to illustrate the demonic opposition to God's plan and this nation. Abraham had to fend them off! Vultures are always present around death!

'As the sun set, Abram fell into a deep sleep, and a thick and dreadful darkness came over him' (Gen. 15:12).

God puts Abram to sleep, instilling fear in him. How can a covenant be made while Abram is unconscious? He must walk through the blood alongside God to partake in the oath. Jesus addresses not just Abram but all His descendants who will come from the promise.

'Then the LORD said to him, *"Know for certain that for four hundred years your descendants will be strangers in a country not their own and that they will be enslaved and mistreated there"* (Gen. 15:13).

This is God talking to Abram's descendants about the future of slavery in Egypt.

But I will punish the nation they serve as slaves, and afterward they will come out with great possessions. You, however, will go to your ancestors in peace and be buried at a good old age. In the fourth generation, your descendants will come back here, for the sin of the Amorites has not yet reached its full measure (Gen. 15:14–16).

God prophesies that certain things must happen, and then His children will return to cleanse the land of wickedness. God is giving the Amorites living there at the time enough rope to hang themselves, as they are heathens. The land needs cleansing because of its evil. Remember, Abram is asleep.

'When the sun had set and darkness had fallen, a smoking fire pot with a blazing torch appeared and passed between the pieces' (Gen. 15:17).

A blazing torch goes down between the pieces, but not Abram.

*'On that day, the LORD made a covenant with Abram and said, "**To your descendants, I give this land, from the Wadi of Egypt to the great river, the Euphrates—**"'* (Gen. 15:18)

The covenant was with God, not Abram and his descendants. God established this promise with Abram, who would uphold the covenant formed prior to the Law of Moses; this vow was made while Abram slept. Furthermore, the promise of the land is significantly more than the land they occupy today.

'The land of the Kenites, Kenizzites, Kadmonites, Hittites, Perizzites, Rephaites, Amorites, Canaanites, Girgashites and Jebusites' (Gen. 15:19–21).

The promise encompasses regions extending from Turkey's borders to the Euphrates River, reaching Saudi Arabia's borders and the Red Sea in Egypt. Currently, they do not possess this. Their present situation reflects the spiritual state of the Jewish nation, as God does not operate in a piecemeal fashion. Nonetheless, they must be in the land for future prophecies to be fulfilled. Some, however, argue that the prophecy was fulfilled when Joshua defeated the land's inhabitants and divided it among the Israelites, as described in Joshua 13. Others also claim it was fulfilled during King David and Solomon's reign, but they never conquered the Hittites in modern-day Turkey to the north of Israel. However, let us turn to Genesis 17, where God reveals to Abram the full extent of the promise.

I will establish my covenant as an everlasting covenant between me and you and your descendants after you for the generations to come, to be your God and the God of your descendants after you. The whole land of Canaan, where you now reside as a foreigner, I will give as an everlasting possession to you and your descendants after you; and I will be their God (Gen. 17:7–8).

An 'everlasting possession.'

This enduring promise will be realised only when Jesus governs during His Millennial Reign here on earth Currently, they possess a fraction of God's initial promise. To clarify, repentance is not required. Since Abram was not included in the original Oath of God regarding the Land, only God passed through the pool of Blood.

This needed to be established before the Law of Moses; otherwise, this promise would have been replaced just like the Law. This paves the way for the promises about Israel's future, as detailed in Daniel 12, which discusses the judgement of Israel and the world in the end times. Israel is not required to repent concerning the land; in fact, they are unable to repent because God has blinded them until *the 'times of the Gentiles are fulfilled'* (Luke 21:24). Here, Gentiles refers to all non-Jews!

Nonetheless, I have come across the idea that modern perspectives claim the Old Testament has become irrelevant after the arrival of Jesus. Therefore, persuading these 'Christians' may prove challenging. Let us examine the Book of Galatians in the New Testament, where Paul confronts false teachings concerning the Law of Moses. Critics questioned his ministry and attempted to sway people to follow the Law.

The promises were spoken to Abraham and his seed. Scripture does not say 'and to seeds,' meaning many people, but 'and to your seed,' meaning one person, Christ. What I mean is this: The law introduced 430 years later does not set aside the covenant previously established by God and thus do away with the promise (Gal. 3:16–17).

The Law of Moses does not nullify the original covenant, which is the Abrahamic Covenant. We proceed to verse 19:

'Why was the law given at all? It was added because of transgressions until the Seed to whom the promise referred had come. The law was given through angels and entrusted to a mediator' (Gal. 3:19).

Here, Paul distinguishes between the Law and the Promise. The Law was given to reveal the nature of sin. The seed mentioned refers to Christ, the great promise alleviates the sting of sin when we accept Him. In Romans, we find a further statement.

'I do not want you to be ignorant of this mystery, brothers and sisters, so that you may not be conceited: Israel has experienced a hardening in part until the full number of the Gentiles has come in' (Rom. 11:25).

Gentiles refer to non-Jews, and God has hardened the hearts of the Jews, making them unable to repent!

And in this way all Israel will be saved. As it is written: 'The deliverer will come from Zion; he will turn godlessness away from Jacob. And this is my covenant with them when I take away their sins.' As far as the gospel is concerned, they are enemies for your sake; but as far as election is concerned, they are loved on account of the patriarchs,' (Rom. 11:26–28).

Once the Church is removed, the Holy Spirit will no longer restrain Satan, allowing him to have his way for a brief period. Jesus will return, and they will see Him whom they have pierced; they will mourn as a mother mourns for her deceased child, and all those who mourn will be saved from it. The promise of the land given to Israel under the Abrahamic Covenant will be fulfilled in the Middle East, far more than it is today.

Let us finally move forwards and see how far the blessing extends in this covenant (Gen. 22:15). Context: God has just asked Abraham, whose name has been changed from Abram, to sacrifice his only son. God stops him and provides a lamb for the sacrifice, but He then says:

The angel of the LORD called to Abraham from heaven a second time and said, 'I swear by myself, declares the LORD, that because you have done this and have not withheld your son, your only son, I will surely bless you and make your descendants as numerous as the stars in the sky and as the sand on the seashore. Your descendants will take possession of the cities of their enemies, and through your offspring all nations on earth will be blessed, because you have obeyed me' (Gen. 22:15–18).

God is now taking another Oath, whose fulfilment is in His hands. The descendants of Abraham will inherit the enemy's cities, and all nations on Earth will be blessed because of your obedience to me.

Ultimately, the earth's most significant gift is the coming of the Lamb provided by God. Abraham's blessing encompasses the promise that all nations will receive blessings through the birth of Jesus, God's Lamb.

So, should we support Israel? Yes, we should. Whatever happens in the current conflict, those who support Israel will be blessed. Hamas and its whole population want the Jews wiped out. People in the United Kingdom who celebrate Hamas have demonstrated their support and have attacked those who support Israel.

Chapter Three - Efforts to Destroy Prophecy

The arrival of Christ on Earth has always been destined to pose a challenge for Satan and the demonic realm. Genesis 3:15 foretells that the seed of the woman would bring about his downfall.

A brief digression! I often ponder why Satan even tries; he is doomed to face the fiery Gehenna, which he dreads. God always speaks the truth and never utters anything He does not mean. Satan believes that if he can thwart God, even in minor ways, and show Him to be false, he can accuse the Lord. This could potentially grant him a reprieve. He focuses on undermining the prophecies found in the Word of God. If those promises can be broken, perhaps the judgement might be overturned. Satan is profoundly misguided! It is remarkable to consider that he was a Guardian Cherub before his fall, as noted in Ezekiel 28. This account highlights the prince of Tyre's pride, wisdom and wealth, as described in the first six verses. The narrative then shifts, and God begins discussing Satan, who influences the King of Tyre. The subsequent verses reveal the reasons behind Satan's fall from grace.

Setting context: In Ezekiel 26, we find a prophecy about the fall of the city of Tyre, located in modern-day Lebanon. The following chapter describes Tyre's immense wealth and magnificence. At the beginning of chapter 28, the Lord addresses 'The King of Tyre', pointing out his pride and vanity regarding what he views as his achievements. This results in judgement, and the Lord declares:

'I will now bring against you a foreign army, the terror of the nations. They will draw their swords against your marvellous wisdom and defile your splendour!' (Ezek. 28:7)

He fails to recognise God as his benefactor; the Lord will bring him down. As you progress through the verses towards the chapter's conclusion, the focus shifts, with God directing His judgement against the demonic influence behind the King of Tyre. He confronts a Guardian Cherub. This chapter of Ezekiel describes a being with immense wisdom and unparalleled beauty. He has been in Eden, the garden of God, and he is adorned with all kinds of precious stones. As the anointed cherub, he has stood on God's holy mountain. This cannot be a human being, which leads me to conclude that it refers to Satan.

'You were anointed as a guardian cherub, so I ordained you. You were on the holy mount of God; you walked among the fiery stones' (Ezek. 28:14).

I have always found it fascinating that Satan served as a Guardian Cherub on God's mountain. However, my companion explained that this role was not intended to safeguard God but to prevent others from approaching Him, as they might be overwhelmed by His presence.

You were blameless in your ways from the day you were created till wickedness was found in you. Through your widespread trade, you were filled with violence, and you sinned. So, I drove you in disgrace from the mount of God and expelled you, guardian cherub, from among the fiery stones. Your heart became proud on account of your beauty, and you corrupted your wisdom because of your splendour. So, I threw you to the earth; I made a spectacle of you before kings. By your many sins and dishonest trade, you have desecrated your sanctuaries. So, I made a fire come out from you, and it consumed you, and I reduced you to ashes on the ground in the sight of all who were watching (Ezek. 28:15–18).

Satan was created perfect, but he became consumed by his beauty; he was corrupted and desired to be like God. He used his influence in Heaven to attract others and aspired to be God because he believed he was like God.

He sought to destroy Israel because he was told that his downfall would come from the Jews. God knew what Satan would attempt, but He had another plan to redeem not only the Jews but all people everywhere who would accept His calling.

The forces of evil, directed by Satan, have relentlessly sought to destroy Israel and the Church throughout the ages, attempting to undermine the promises of God. When Christ was crucified, he may have believed that victory was within his grasp—until Jesus was raised from the dead and the Church came into being. Through God's Holy Word, Satan realised that once the 'times of the Gentiles are fulfilled,' this would signal his end during the latter days.

Our church fathers might be partially justified in believing that the Church had replaced the Jews, as there was no 'Israel' for 2,000 years. The Jewish people had been expelled from their homeland and dispersed globally, giving rise to 'antisemitism.' Consequently, the promises made to Israel were reassigned to the Church, and the prophetic texts in the Bible were allegorised to fit this perspective, a belief that persists today. Nevertheless, Christians can no longer dismiss the Jews. Their return to the Land has triggered the fulfilment of God's prophetic Word concerning Israel, the Land, and, most crucially, their redemption. Considering the initial part of this narrative, all prophecies in the Bible are intricately linked to Israel. When the disciples, who were Jews, asked Jesus about the 'signs of the end of the age,' He gave them answers.

'Now learn this lesson from the fig tree: As soon as its twigs get tender and its leaves come out, you know that summer is near. Even so, when you see all these things, you know that it is near, right at the door' (Matt. 24:32–33).

Chapter Four - Lesson of the Fig Tree

Before we proceed, let us clarify the meaning behind the fig tree reference. In the Bible, God uses symbols like grapes, vines and figs to depict the spiritual state of people, nations or situations. Jesus Himself referred to 'fruit' to signify a person's life and development. He mentions the vine to illustrate His nature and curses the fig tree, which we explored in Luke 13.

The statement 'I am the True Vine' (John 15:1) represents the final of Jesus' 'I am' affirmations found in John's Gospel. These statements illuminate His distinct divine identity and mission. Spoken to His closest friends just before Judas' betrayal (John 13:30), Jesus declared, 'I am the True Vine.' The Lord prepared the disciples for His crucifixion, resurrection and upcoming ascension to Heaven.

The olives, figs and vine trees list the rights God offers to Israel.

The olive tree symbolises Israel's religious rights, through which they received the Law and the Prophets (Jeremiah 11). The flowering olive tree represents beauty and abundance in the Bible. From the olive tree comes the oil of anointing.

The Fig Tree symbolises Israel's national rights, encompassing the twelve tribes and land allocation. In Jeremiah 24:1–7, the LORD presented Jeremiah with two baskets of figs in front of the temple. One basket held good figs, while the other contained bad figs. The good figs represented the Jewish exiles in Babylon who were taken from the Land.

He also bestowed upon them the privilege of a personal relationship with Him, represented by the Vine. The Vine signifies Israel's honour in worshipping God at the temple, enabling a connection with Him. This is depicted in Psalm 80:8–11. This psalm is a cry to restore His face to them.

'You transplanted a vine from Egypt; you drove out the nations and planted it' (Ps. 80:8).

Jesus is now our vine. We are temples of the Holy Spirit and enjoy direct access to God through Jesus, our High Priest. When He communicated with us, Jesus used the vine as a metaphor to illustrate our relationship with Him and our success, measured by the fruit we bear.

The fig tree mentioned in Matthew 24:32 symbolises Israel, with Jesus highlighting its significance in the subsequent verse. Israel's national privilege, as outlined in the Abrahamic Covenant, began to be renewed in 1948 when the nation reestablished itself. However, this restoration represents only a part of the original promise due to its current spiritual condition. Jesus notes that when these events occur, His prophecies in Matthew, particularly in chapters 24 and 25, will be fulfilled.

This indicates that when Israel was established as a nation and returned to its land, the prophetic clock restarted, heralding the emergence of signs indicating the end of the age. It is important to note that the initial promise of land was broader than what they currently hold. Israel's return to the land shows us the next peak in our journey.

For centuries, Israel existed as an unseen nation, lacking a government, territory, temple or priesthood, as well as any signs of national existence. Its people were scattered worldwide. In 1948, Israel reestablished itself as a nation, complete with its land, government, currency and particularly the language, which devoted individuals preserved. Spiritually, the nation remains desolate and unfruitful for God. Nevertheless, regarding national life, we might observe that its branches appear green and tender.

The fig tree is a fitting emblem of Israel. Its peculiarity is that the fruit blossoms appear before the leaves. Therefore, we should look for fruit on a fully leafed tree. This explains why Jesus cursed the fig tree with only leaves (Matthew 21:18–20). Seeing the leaves, He anticipated fruit, and when none appeared, He cursed the tree for being barren. Mark offers a different perspective on this event in Mark 11:12–14, noting that Jesus discovered only leaves, 'for the time of figs had not yet come.' So why did He curse the tree?

Early fruits or blossoms emerge from the previous year's growth in spring, having survived the winter. By June—or sometimes even earlier—the fruit for that season is ready for harvest. In contrast, unripe autumn fruit from the previous year often withstands winter and ripens as spring growth begins anew. It was early April when Jesus cursed the fig tree; it was not yet the season for figs, which typically appear in June. However, fig trees that retain their leaves through winter usually bear some of last year's figs, and April is too early for new leaves or fruit. Knowing this, Jesus, upon seeing leaves on the tree, expected to find some of last year's crop.

Let us utilise this to illustrate the fig tree and Israel's present status in the prophecy timeline.

'Now learn this lesson from the fig tree: As soon as its twigs get tender and its leaves come out, you know that summer is near' (Matt. 24:32).

This mirrors Luke 21:29–30 and Mark 13:28. The leaves are budding, and the twigs are tender, yet there is no fruit because summer has not yet arrived, and none remain from the previous season—no fruit in Israel. Spiritually, the nation remains barren and cold; there is no fruit for God. However, on a national level, we might say that its branches are green and tender. This reflects the current state of Israel. There is no fruit, but the twigs and leaves are fresh. They are worldly, lacking spiritual fruit, yet increasingly prosperous and wealthier with each passing season. With the arrival of summer and the Lord's return to Earth at the end of this age, they will see Him whom they have pierced, leading to the salvation of all Israel. It is then that we shall witness the new fruit.

Chapter Five - The Current Situation

The wars in Israel, which began even before the land was granted to them in 1948, have always posed a threat. This period is detailed in Psalm 83, which prophesies ongoing troubles for Israel to the present day. I will address this Psalm later; however, the animosity extends back to the time of Abraham. Abraham's mistake in fathering Ishmael endures. Some errors do not impact others, yet we sometimes make choices that disrupt the status quo. Satan has taken advantage of this to create demonic opposition to God's plan for a Saviour.

Ishmael's descendants continue to pose a threat to Israel, leading us to review a ruling rendered by God directed at Hagar, Ishmael's mother, detailing his character. Within Islamic tradition, Ishmael is regarded as the heir, taking Isaac's place and viewed as the true 'Son of the Promise,' being firstborn. This ongoing conflict traces back to Ishmael and involves Esau's lineage. Let us delve deeper into this topic. In the end, God reveals the essence of Ishmael.

Abraham is honoured as a remarkable figure and called righteous. This is confirmed in the Book of

James: '*Abraham believed God, and it was credited to him as righteousness*' (James 2:23). This should instil hope, as he faced challenges in life just like we do. Now, let us delve into his story and God's purpose.

Abraham's ancestry plays a vital role in Christianity. The world's Saviour is born through him and his son, Isaac (Matthew 1; Luke 3). We can draw lessons from his journey as a devoted believer in God, even during moments of doubt. By Abraham's time, humanity had wholly turned away from God, had been destroyed by a flood (except for Noah and his family), and was once more turning away from God. In Genesis 11, we see the Tower of Babel, which was built to reach the heavens and worship other gods.

God summoned Abram (as he was called then) from his family to fulfil His purpose of creating a nation for Himself. His father, Terah, a pagan priest, originally gave him the name Abram, but God later changed it to Abraham. The name Abram means 'exalted father,' a title given to him by his father to honour himself. In contrast, the name Abraham translates to 'father of nations.' In Genesis 17, God made a covenant with Abraham.

When Abram was ninety-nine years old, the LORD appeared to him and said, 'I am God Almighty; walk before me faithfully and be blameless. Then I will make my covenant between me and you and will greatly increase your numbers.' Abram fell facedown, and God said to him, 'As for me, this is my covenant with you: You will be the father of many nations. No longer will you be called Abram; your name will be Abraham, for I have made you a father of many nations. I will make you exceedingly fruitful; I will make nations of you, and kings will come from you (Gen. 17:1–6).

The Lord changed His name, symbolising a rebirth into a new identity and selected this individual to establish a nation for Himself, showcasing the blessings that come to those who follow Him and adhere to His laws. Now, we will explore Abraham's character, acknowledging his greatness while noting his vulnerabilities.

As recorded, God guided Abraham towards the Holy Land, where he was chosen to be the father of many nations, including the Jewish nation, which was ultimately given the Laws of God. Together with his wife, Sarah, he taught people about the existence of one God who cannot be seen. His legacy was carried on by his son, Isaac, whom he almost sacrificed at God's command. The first of the patriarchs is referred to by Jewish people as Avraham Avinu, meaning 'Abraham our father.' Abraham was born and raised in Ur of the Chaldees, in modern-day Iraq, near Nasiriyah in the country's southeastern part.

Joshua 24:2 says that Abraham and his father worshipped idols. Let us go to Joshua 24:1–3. Setting the scene, Joshua is about to die, and he summons the people, warning them about the sovereignty of God.

Joshua said to all the people, 'This is what the LORD, the God of Israel, says: "Long ago your ancestors, including Terah the father of Abraham and Nahor, lived beyond the Euphrates River and worshipped other gods. But I took your father Abraham from the land beyond the Euphrates and led him throughout Canaan and gave him many descendants. I gave him Isaac"' (Josh. 24:2–3).

God took Abraham, led him across the River Euphrates, and guided him toward the land He was about to promise him. When Abraham crossed the river, he became a Hebrew but never a Jew. 'Hebrew' means one who crosses over. He transitioned from an idol worshipper to crossing the water and becoming a Hebrew. We should also note that he never became a Jew.

Some facts about Abraham:

Abraham was already old when God called him to leave his home and promised him a son. He was nearly 100 when he and Sarah had Isaac. God had called him twenty-five years earlier.

The Lord instructed Abraham to leave his father's household and journey to a new land he would inherit. Abraham showed great faith, setting out in obedience to God, even though he never received the promised land. He lived as a nomad, continually travelling from place to place. The only land he owned was a burial site—a cave in a field that he purchased from the Hittites to bury Sarah when she passed away.

Abraham made significant mistakes and did not seem to learn from them. While travelling, he let two kings think that Sarah was his sister (Genesis 12 and 20), conveniently omitting that she was his wife to avoid danger. He acted out of fear. The kings desired her because of her beauty. Fortunately, God intervened, and both kings discovered the truth, allowing Sarah to be returned to him. We find that Abraham, known as a friend of God, was just as prone to fear and deceit as we are, even though he knew God was with him. As I pointed out, this should encourage us because he did not lead a sinless life, not that we should use this as a 'get out of jail free' card.

In summary, following the flood and during Abraham's era, humanity once again turned away from God, as shown by the Tower of Babel in Genesis 11. A tower was built reaching towards the heavens, leading mankind to worship other deities. The Lord intervened by creating confusion among them, resulting in different languages and making communication difficult. Consequently, people separated into groups, seeking those with whom they could communicate. This laid the groundwork for nations, impeding the advancement of evil by complicating communication and fragmenting humanity.

God called Abraham away from his family to initiate His plan to establish a nation for Himself, demonstrating to the world through this nation the blessings available to those who follow Him and obey His laws. God promised Abraham that He would make him a blessing to the world through an heir, despite Sarah's advanced age.

Abraham was seventy-five years old when he first received the promise, and Genesis 21:5 tells us he was nearly 100 when Isaac was born. Sarah was ninety. Abraham and Sarah waited twenty-five years for God's promise to manifest. In the meantime, Abraham tried to help God solve this problem because he was elderly and could not father a son. Let us look at Genesis 16:1–2.

Now Sarai, Abram's wife, had borne him no children. But she had an Egyptian slave named Hagar; so she said to Abram, 'The LORD has kept me from having children. Go, sleep with my slave; perhaps I can build a family through her.' Abram agreed to what Sarai said (Gen. 16:1–2).

Now, you might view this as something a Godly man would not do, and yes, adultery is a sin, even with Sarah's consent. However, it was customary at that time. Abraham came from a pagan background, and in that society, it would not have been illegal for a man to have children with another woman if his wife could not conceive; the primary goal was to have a son and heir to his father's house. Thus, Abraham sinned, and Ishmael was born, causing ongoing trouble to this day.

Abraham and his wife, Sarah, had long desired a child. As they aged—Abraham was eighty-six and Sarah was seventy-six—they felt they needed to help God. Together, they decided that Abraham should have a child with Sarah's servant, Hagar, leading to the birth of Ishmael. This caused significant strife between Hagar and Sarah. Ultimately, as described in the Old Testament, Abraham sent Hagar away after God revealed that the promise was not meant for Ishmael's descendants. Soon after Abraham had relations with Hagar, she became pregnant and mocked Sarah. This was unbearable for Sarah, as mentioned in Genesis 16:5:

'Then Sarai told Abram, "You are responsible for the wrong I am suffering. I put my slave in your arms, and now that she knows she is pregnant, she despises me. May the LORD judge between you and me."'

Sarah blames Abraham even though it was her idea. Now, we are examining the age-old trouble the Jewish nation has endured over the centuries. This issue did not begin in 1948, when they returned to the land. The problem emerged with the birth of Isaac. Ishmael became jealous of Isaac when he was born. God speaks of Ishmael.

'He will be a wild donkey of a man; his hand will be against everyone and everyone's hand against him, and he will live in hostility toward all his brothers' (Gen. 16:12).

God blessed Hagar with a son and promised that her descendants would be too numerous to count. You will discover that twelve nations come from Ishmael if you read on. Nevertheless, in verse 12, we see the character of this man, which would carry over to his offspring. Ishmael would be a '*wild man with his hand against every man and every man's hand against him,*' a trait of Ishmael's and Esau's (Ishmael's son-in-law and Jacob's brother) descendants to the present time.

At a feast for Isaac some fourteen years later, Ishmael began to reveal the nature God said he would have by mocking and ridiculing his little half-brother. He viewed him as a usurper, and this mindset endures throughout his lineage. By this time, Sarah had grown weary of Hagar and her son, demanding that Abraham expel them from the household and asserting that the son of a slave would not be his heir. God also confirmed this. The fallout from this has persisted through the ages, laying the groundwork for conflict with the nations of the Middle East.

Genesis 21 states that God was with Ishmael, and as he grew up in the wilderness, he became skilled with a bow. His mother arranged for him to marry a wife from

Egypt. Ishmael fathered twelve sons and a daughter who married Esau (Genesis 28:9; 36:2–3). He lived to the ripe old age of 137. Scripture notes that Ishmael's numerous descendants settled near the eastern border of Egypt. Trouble also came from the line of Esau!

The Arab nations claim to be descendants of Ishmael and possess significantly more land than Israel; yet for them, it all ties back to the birthright. They continue to believe that Ishmael was the firstborn child of Abraham and, as such, are entitled to everything. This sin of Abraham has caused trouble throughout the ages and will persist until Jesus returns to rule and reign. We see that the great man Abraham was truly faithful to God. However, we sometimes try to help God achieve things, which can lead us to error or sin, as it is part of our nature. I want to address just one thing before we move on.

Abraham and Sarah were relatives, and the Bible states that God forbade intermarriage among relatives when Israel was established as a nation and given the Law. Returning to Adam and Eve, we see they were close relatives because God took Eve from Adam's side. It is essential to recall that Adam and Eve's sons and daughters were the first to inhabit the Earth. At that time, their genes were pure. Indeed, Adam and Eve were, but as the population began to grow, the effects of sin caused genetic alterations. Later, it became risky for families to intermarry, as this would increase the likelihood of generational issues. One reason incest is so strongly discouraged in the world today is that reproduction between closely related individuals carries a significantly higher risk of genetic irregularities. However, this was not a concern in the early days of humanity because human DNA was relatively defect-free. Abraham's marriage to his half-sister, Sarah, would have been encouraged as it was within their family or tribe, and no one would have found it unusual. God clarified this later in Leviticus 18, as sin affected mankind's genes, and close relatives would only increase the likelihood of defects in their descendants.

Chapter Six - Psalm 83

Now, we come to a crucial aspect of this prophetic narrative. Since its establishment in 1948, Israel has been at war, enduring numerous conflicts with various Arab forces, including those in 1948–49, 1956, 1967, 1973, 1982, 2006, and the ongoing clashes up to the present. While other exchanges have occurred, the ones mentioned are the primary ones. The title of this chapter provides a clue to the conflict in Israel that has persisted since ancient times.

Psalm 83 is a lament regarding an alliance of nations conspiring to destroy Israel and its legacy. This psalm was written by a prophet named Asaph. He is recognised in twelve psalms and is said to be the son of Berechiah, a progenitor of the Asaphites, one of the groups of musicians in the First Temple. He is the author of Psalm 83. The conflicts mentioned in this psalm have persisted for centuries. However, could its conclusion be unfolding in our generation? The clue lies in the nations referenced within the psalm. This psalm seems to address contemporary issues in the Middle East—nations conspiring to destroy Israel.

When searching for these modern nations, we encounter difficulty identifying them all.

We know that Assyria is in modern-day Iraq and that the Ishmaelites descended from Abraham and Hagar, from whom the Arabs claim descent. In the Bible, we can trace the Edomites and Amalekites, who descended from Esau, and the Moabites and Ammonites, who descended from Lot. However, tracing them today is nearly impossible.

The Philistines inhabited the area now known as the Gaza Strip, while the city of Tyre is in present-day Lebanon. Some sources identify the Hagrites as descendants of Hagar and, thus, part of the Ishmaelites; however, this identification remains somewhat unclear. Given the ambiguity surrounding these names, it suffices to view them as representing the Gentile foes of Israel, and the psalm should be applied accordingly. It is essential to highlight that the psalm was not created during wartime. About 3,000 years ago, Asaph, King David's worship leader, composed it during a time of significant prosperity, freedom and peace. Therefore, the setting of this psalm is in a time of peace, but Asaph anticipated future challenges!

With cunning, they conspire against your people; they plot against those you cherish. 'Come,' they say, 'let us destroy them as a nation so that Israel's name is remembered no more.' With one mind, they plot together; they form an alliance against you— (Ps. 83:3–5)

That is the battle cry of every nation surrounding Israel today. This 'Ring of Fire' encircles Israel with Hezbollah in Lebanon, Hamas in Gaza, and Islamic Jihad (including foreign militias in Syria, distant Iraq, and Yemen), with Iran pulling the strings. At its rebirth in 1948, war erupted when five Arab nations invaded the territory immediately after the announcement of the state of Israel on 14 May. Conspiring against the Jewish people is not new. From the Philistines during the time of King David to the Nazis, the Jewish people have faced plots against them.

'See how your enemies growl, how your foes rear their heads. With cunning, they conspire against your people; they plot against those you cherish' (Ps. 83:2–3).

This age-old psalm expresses a cry against God's people, from King David to modern-day Israel. Its conclusion will come when the Church is removed. Then Jesus returns with us and will rule and reign in Jerusalem. In the psalm, Asaph's petition to God is for the intervention and protection of Israel from its enemies.

Verses 6–8: Ten nations form a coalition against Israel.

Verses 9–12: Asaph is assured that God will fight on Israel's side.

Verses 13–17: He asks God to make Israel's enemies suffer.

In conclusion, we can relate this ancient psalm from King David's reign to today's context. Israel seemed absent from the world stage for 2,000 years, but now we witness its dramatic revival. The recent strikes against Israel are unlike anything seen before. Several missile attacks that would have crippled other nations in the Middle East have had minimal impact on Israel.

'"Come," they say, "let us destroy them as a nation, so that Israel's name is remembered no more"' (Ps. 83:4).

This is the age-old cry of Ishmael. So, what will the outcome of this current conflict be?

Chapter Seven - At the Door

God tells us that He makes His plans known to us. In Isaiah, He says:

'I make known the end from the beginning, from ancient times, what is still to come. I say, "My purpose will stand, and I will do all I please"' (Isa. 46:10).

As the Book of Revelation mentions, the Lord has declared that Israel will ultimately have peace. Citing the 'Hill and Valley principle,' the mountain is in sight. When we examine the scene, we notice the ongoing conflict in Israel, prompting us to consider that they have predominantly experienced war since 1948. These are part of the 'Wars and Rumours of Wars' spoken of by Jesus to His disciples. However, we have not seen the destruction and chaos mentioned in Revelation or Daniel 12. Eventually, peace will prevail on Earth, with Jesus reigning from Jerusalem. This will take place once He establishes His kingdom here and confines Satan. What should we expect soon? Unfulfilled prophecies can offer insight. The chapter title, 'At the Door,' comes from Mark 13:28–29.

"Now learn this lesson from the fig tree: As soon as its twigs get tender and its leaves come out, you know that summer is near. Even so, when you see these things happening, you know that it is near, right ***at the door****"* (Mark 13:28–29).

Also see Matthew 24:32 and Luke 21:29–30.

All three references pertain to the fig tree, which we associate with Israel. The leaves are soft and newly emerged, the twigs are lush and green, yet fruit is absent. This symbolises Israel's present condition: it is physically flourishing but spiritually barren due to a lack of spiritual development. They possess only a small part of the original promise, mirroring Israel's spiritual state; they cannot fully comprehend it without national repentance. What does it signify when summer approaches and is nearly upon us? Luke explains this in the very next verse!

'Even so, when you see these things happening, you know that the kingdom of God is near' (Luke 21:31).

This signifies that Jesus is at the door and that the age of wickedness is approaching its end, when He will establish His kingdom here on Earth. He also states that the people living during that time, both older and younger, will witness all of these events.

"Truly I tell you, this generation will certainly not pass away until all these things have happened. Heaven

and earth will pass away, but my words will never pass away" (Luke 21:32–33).

Now, refrain from concentrating on the word 'generation'. Some try to define the duration of a generation in years. However, that is not the implication here. It signifies that those living at that time will witness all these events. It must occur in Judea with the Jews having returned to the land, as Jesus refers to a specific horror where something unholy has taken place.

'"So when you see standing in the holy place 'the abomination that causes desolation,' spoken of through the prophet Daniel—let the reader understand—"' (Matt. 24:15).

This event aligns with the description given by the prophet Daniel. By looking closely at Daniel 9:27, we can understand Jesus' references and demonstrate that all these events take place in Israel.

He will confirm a covenant with many for one "seven." In the middle of the "seven", he will put an end to sacrifice and offering. And at the temple, he will set up an abomination that causes desolation, until the end that is decreed is poured out on him (Dan. 9:27).

Part of the current Jewish community plans to construct a temple exclusively in Jerusalem, on the original site, for performing sacrifices and offerings.

This will take place in a rebuilt temple located in Jerusalem. I will discuss this verse later; for now, it is enough to say that this is what Jesus alludes to.

'Then let those who are in Judea flee to the mountains' (Matt. 24:16).

See also this verse:

'Pray that your flight will not take place in winter or on the Sabbath' (Matt. 24:20).

He references the Sabbath, indicating a discussion about the Jews in Judea, whom He advises to escape. He repeatedly warns them not to be deceived by false claimants to the title of Messiah, as He is the true Messiah. The Jews persist in seeking the Messiah due to their rejection of Jesus, which leaves them vulnerable to falsehoods. This caution is not relevant to Christians, who acknowledge Jesus as the Messiah, while non-believers generally remain indifferent.

When the fig tree begins to blossom, it signifies Israel's return to the land: robust, prosperous, well-equipped to defend itself, yet spiritually lifeless. Jesus states He is at the door. He urges them to flee because trouble is near. This abomination established in the temple triggers the judgements in Revelation that precede the actual second coming of Jesus. God is furious about this abomination. These Jews have built a temple that He did not command them to construct. They have allowed an idol in this rebuilt temple. Extremists are worshipping Satan, though they may not realise it.

Jesus had previously discussed the signs of the end of the age. He said, 'No one knows the day or the hour.' This cannot refer to a specific point during the Great Tribulation period, as the worldwide carnage would alert us all. Jesus notes that it will be like the days of Noah. Noah preached the message that God was going to destroy the world. He built a massive ship on a mountain and must have faced questioning and mockery. God took Noah and placed him in the Ark with his family; He sealed them tightly inside and flooded the world. Furthermore, Jesus states, 'One will be taken and another left.' As in Noah's day, those who love the Lord will be shielded as God judges the world.

While those living, before Christ returns for His bride, will be unaware of the exact day or hour, individuals who understand prophecy and endure the great tribulation will witness significant events. Should any remain on Earth when He comes for the Bride, God forbid, seeking the Word will become essential. Grasping His teachings will aid in interpreting the unfolding events. This event will occur three and a half years after the idol is established in the temple (totalling 1,260 days). God has revealed these specific days to us!

The Jewish calendar is a combination of a lunar calendar and a solar calendar. Without elaborating too much, the 360-day year was convenient in ancient times because it was connected to the length of daylight, the visibility of the moon and the length of shadows. Therefore, using this as a base to calculate the relationship to 1,260 days reveals that it amounts to three and a half years. Recall 'context and culture.'

Revelation 11 reveals that significant events will occur, observable to the world. God appoints two witnesses to proclaim the gospel message while confronting Satan and his demons.

And I will appoint my two witnesses, and they will prophesy for 1,260 days, clothed in sackcloth.' They are 'the two olive trees' and the two lampstands, and 'they stand before the Lord of the earth.' If anyone tries to harm them, fire comes from their mouths and devours their enemies. This is how anyone who wants to harm them must die (Rev. 11:3–5).

This cannot be hidden. The world is in trouble, and inexplicable miracles are happening. How on earth has a temple been built in Jerusalem? Something must have caused this change.

The location of the next temple in Jerusalem remains uncertain. The site is a focal point of the modern conflict between Arabs, especially Muslims and Israelis. It houses the Dome of the Rock, an Islamic shrine, and the Al-Aqsa Mosque—another significant Islamic site.

According to Scripture, another temple in Jerusalem will offer sacrifices. Currently, the Temple Institute and other movements aim to build the Third Temple on the Temple Mount. God does not sanction this! For another temple to be constructed at its original location, the existing Muslim shrine must be demolished to make way for the new structure. How might the Muslims react to that? For this to occur, some peace must be fostered between Muslims, Jews and the surrounding nations.

This peace will be established through a treaty within a specific period, as recorded by the prophet, Daniel, in Daniel 9:27. Let us provide the context for this verse. Daniel petitioned God because he recognised, from studying Jeremiah, that Jerusalem would remain desolate for seventy years during his lifetime, and that time is nearly up!

Chapter Eight - Peace

Israel has undoubtedly not known peace since 1948 when it returned to the land. However, according to Scripture, peace will precede Jesus' establishment of His kingdom. Given the ongoing conflict in the Middle East against Israel, this seems impossible. Is peace attainable? Let us explore the scriptures, starting with Jesus' warning to those residing in Judea during a specific time in the future.

Before we proceed, we need to establish a framework based on this mystery. We will consult the following prophets from the Old Testament regarding their connection to Jesus' discourse in Matthew 24 and the Book of Revelation, which concludes the discussion of future events concerning the end of time. Jesus is the link to all that we discuss. The Old Testament prophets we will consult to set this framework are Daniel, mentioned by Jesus, Jeremiah, mentioned by Daniel, and Ezekiel, a contemporary of Jeremiah. The end of Ezekiel 36 is prophetic concerning Israel, referring to God's promise to put a new Spirit into His people.

Ezekiel and Daniel lived during the same period and were likely of similar ages. Ezekiel prophesied in Babylon while Daniel served in the Babylonian government and resided in the palace. Both Ezekiel and Jeremiah conveyed similar messages, particularly the assertion that God's remnant included the exiles in Babylon (Ezekiel 20:40, Jeremiah 31:7). Jeremiah remained in Jerusalem when Ezekiel was taken and continued to prophesy to the remaining Jews. Thus, they all existed in the same era but were in different locations. Finally, in 2 Thessalonians, Paul mentions a man of lawlessness who establishes an idol.

'He will oppose and will exalt himself over everything that is called God or is worshipped, so that he sets himself up in God's temple, proclaiming himself to be God' (2 Thess. 2:4).

To begin, here is a quotation by Jesus concerning the prophet, Daniel. According to Matthew 24:

So when you see standing in the holy place 'the abomination that causes desolation,' spoken of through the prophet Daniel—let the reader understand—then let those who are in Judea flee to the mountains. Let no one on the housetop go down to take anything out of the house. Let no one in the field return to get their cloak (Matt. 24:15–18).

Jesus commands, 'Flee!' At the time of this prophecy, the Jews still lived in Israel. The temple had not yet fallen, yet Jesus predicted its destruction at the beginning of chapter 24. Historical accounts show that the temple was destroyed around AD 70. From Christ's time until the temple's demise, there are no historical records of any abomination mentioned by Jesus in this passage. Eventually, the Jews were expelled from their land and dispersed throughout the known world. Thus, this abomination must occur after the temple's destruction, requiring another 'holy place' to be rebuilt.

Only one 'period of peace' is described for Israel in the Old Testament—Daniel 9, where a man confirms a covenant. Let us turn to Daniel 9:27. We reference Daniel because Jesus explicitly connects the future to Daniel's prophecy and these scriptures.

He will confirm a covenant with many for one 'seven.' In the middle of the 'seven', he will put an end to sacrifice and offering. And at the temple, he will set up an abomination that causes desolation, until the end that is decreed is poured out on him (Dan. 9:27).

First, we should acknowledge that Daniel 9:24–27 is a profound mystery that has sparked countless discussions and interpretations. It directly refers to the Messiah as 'the anointed one.' The connection lies in Daniel discussing Jesus (the anointed one), who in turn quotes Daniel. Let us establish the context for Daniel 9. He is among the exiled Jews who did not reside in the land. King Nebuchadnezzar captured some and took them to Babylon following his assault on Jerusalem during the third year of Jehoiakim's reign. Daniel reads the Book of Jeremiah and realises that the seventy years of exile are approaching their end.

In the first year of Darius, son of Xerxes (a Mede by descent), who was made ruler over the Babylonian kingdom—in the first year of his reign, I, Daniel, understood from the Scriptures, according to the word of the LORD given to Jeremiah the prophet, that the desolation of Jerusalem would last seventy years (Dan. 9:1–2).

So, he takes the scripture literally and starts to pray!

'So I turned to the Lord God and pleaded with him in prayer and petition, in fasting, and in sackcloth and ashes' (Dan. 9:3).

In verses 24–27, the angel Gabriel responds to his prayer, delivering more than he expected. This passage is divided into three sections, beginning with the angel Gabriel's message in verse 24. (Jesus quotes from verse 27.)

Seventy 'sevens' are decreed for your people and your holy city to finish transgression, to put an end to sin, to atone for wickedness, ***to bring in everlasting righteousness****, to seal up vision and prophecy and to anoint the Most Holy Place* (Dan. 9:24).

To bring about eternal righteousness, which has yet to occur! Gabriel refers to you and your people, specifically the Jewish community. The 'seventy-sevens' or 'seventy weeks,' as noted in certain translations, signify periods that achieve these results:

- 'To finish transgression'
- 'To put an end to sin'
- 'To atone for wickedness'
- 'To bring in everlasting righteousness'
- 'To seal up vision and prophecy'
- 'To anoint the most holy'

This ends sin! The 'Anointed One' will accomplish all this. When He comes to rule and reign on Earth, there will be peace for 1,000 years during the millennium referred to in Revelation 19:1–3.

And I saw an angel coming down out of heaven, having the key to the Abyss and holding in his hand a great chain. He seized the dragon, that ancient serpent, who is the devil, or Satan, and bound him for a thousand years. He threw him into the Abyss and locked and sealed it over him to keep him from deceiving the nations anymore until the thousand years were ended. After that, he must be set free for a short time (Rev. 20:1–3).

The only way true peace sanctioned by God can be established here on the earth is with Satan locked away. Next verse, Daniel 9:25:

Know and understand this: From the time the word goes out to restore and rebuild Jerusalem until the

Anointed One, the ruler, comes, there will be seven 'sevens,' and sixty-two 'sevens.' It will be rebuilt with streets and a trench in times of trouble (Dan. 9:25).

'Sevens.' What does it signify? In Judaism, seven is considered perfect, symbolising perfection or divine wholeness. The Bible is filled with references to seven, appearing several hundred times throughout the Old and New Testaments. Therefore, seventy sevens will fulfil God's will, including the anointing of Jesus as the Holy One. What do these seventy sevens represent? God establishes a time frame through the angel Gabriel to end sin and introduce righteousness. Can we determine how long this will take? We have what seems to be a period of seventy-sevens, which is divided into two parts:

1. First, 'a' seven (this is the answer to Daniel's prayer)
2. Then 'sixty-two' sevens (to Messiah or anointed one)

This makes sixty-nine sevens (7 + 62).

In the *NKJV*, it reads:

Seventy weeks *are determined for your people and for your holy city, to finish the transgression, to make an end of sins, to make reconciliation for iniquity, to bring in everlasting righteousness, to seal up vision and prophecy, and to anoint the Most Holy* (Dan. 9:24).

The *NKJV* uses *'weeks'* instead of *'sevens.'* However, it cannot mean weeks because everything still needs to be completed; that duration is too short. It could even mean years! We gain insight from John 2:22. Let us establish the context.

As a devout Jew, the Lord Jesus went to Jerusalem to celebrate Passover, a significant day on the Jewish calendar. Upon arriving at the temple, he found it transformed into a marketplace. Oxen, sheep and doves were for sale, and money changers were conducting business. Jesus caused a commotion by overturning tables and driving out the animals. They questioned His authority; to Jesus, it resembled a den of robbers and thieves!

'So the Jews answered and said to Him, *"What sign do You show to us since You do these things?"'* (John 2:18)

The conclusion is clear: demonstrate that you have the authority to take this action! Jesus then responds:

'Jesus answered and said to them, "Destroy this temple, and in three days I will raise it up"' (John 2:19).

That amazed them, *but* He was talking about His body.

'Then the Jews said, *"It has taken forty-six years to build this temple, and will You raise it in three days?"'* (John 2:20).

We have a clue. The temple in Jerusalem took forty-six years to rebuild. Gabriel discusses Jerusalem's restoration in 'One Seven,' which connects it to the sabbath years. The seventh year is a sabbath year of rest for the land. The Jews were required to cultivate the land for six years and let it rest in the seventh. This cycle of seven years answers Daniel's prayer. Let us explore this land's sabbath.

Six years you shall sow your field, and six years you shall prune your vineyard, and gather its fruit; but in the seventh year, there shall be a sabbath of solemn rest for the land, a sabbath to the LORD. You shall neither sow your field nor prune your vineyard (Lev. 25:3–4).

At the time of Daniel's prophecy, the Jews were not in the land. God drove them out because they had not kept the sabbath for the land.

'The land enjoyed its sabbath rests; all the time of its desolation it rested, until the seventy years were completed in fulfilment of the word of the LORD spoken by Jeremiah' (2 Chr. 36:21).

The Jews disobeyed God's command concerning the Sabbath. After residing in the Promised Land for about 800 years, they neglected His Sabbath rest for 490 years, corresponding to seventy cycles of seven years. The Sabbath rest occurred every seventh day and every seventh year, necessitating a break from work each week and an uncultivated year for the land every seven years. God instituted this practice to allow the land to recover while emphasising the importance of trust and obedience. The Jewish people manifested their faith in God's provision by refraining from agricultural activities for an entire year. Judgement was foretold for those who transgressed God's Sabbath rest.

So, these 'sevens' refer to when people were expelled from the land for failing to observe the Sabbath Law regarding the land, which also included forgiving debts. This would have significantly eased the burden for those struggling with debt! At the end of every seven years, you shall grant a remission of debts.

At the end of every seven years you must cancel debts. This is how it is to be done: Every creditor shall cancel any loan they have made to a fellow Israelite. They shall not require payment from anyone among their own people, because the LORD's time for cancelling debts has been proclaimed (Deut. 15:1–2).

Debts must be cancelled at the end of every seven years, including accrued interest. They had not observed the Sabbath of the Land for 490 years. Daniel's prophecy amounts to 490 years or seventy 'land' sabbaths. The restoration of the Second Temple, including Jerusalem, took forty-nine years, or 'one seven.' During the rebuilding of this temple, they faced significant opposition. However, it took forty-six years to complete the temple, as noted in John 2:24. The additional three years were for the reconstruction of Jerusalem and the opposition they encountered (Ezra 4).

In summary, they had failed to observe the Sabbath Law of the Land for 490 years, which is related to their neglect of seventy years of sabbaths, or 'seventy-sevens.'

We have established that it took forty-nine years to rebuild Jerusalem, including the temple. Therefore, the following sixty-two sevens signify years and prophecies concerning the Messiah's presence on Earth and His being 'cut off' or killed.

After the sixty-two 'sevens,' the Anointed One will be put to death and will have nothing. The people of the ruler who will come will destroy the city and the sanctuary. The end will come like a flood: War will continue until the end, and desolations have been decreed (Dan. 9:26).

Many have attempted to calculate when Jesus was killed, but this is not my focus. What I am addressing is a false period of peace on Earth, NOT established by God. This can be found in the last set of seven, where a covenant is made between a man, 'many,' and Israel, as in Daniel 9:27. This last set of seven represents the final seven years of the seventy-sevens mentioned by Gabriel, God's messenger. This period marks the time of the Great Tribulation that will come at the end of this age.

He will confirm a covenant with many for one 'seven.' In the middle of the 'seven', he will put an end to sacrifice and offering. And at the temple, he will set up an abomination that causes desolation, until the end that is decreed is poured out on him (Dan. 9:27).

A 'covenant' is confirmed! This respected leader successfully brokered peace for the Jewish people in the Middle East through a covenant. However, midway through, he halts the sacrifices. The Jewish community will not offer sacrifices to God unless a temple is reconstructed on the Temple Mount in Old Jerusalem. Inside this temple, a figure establishes what Gabriel calls an 'abomination.' This may be an idol positioned at the heart of the temple, known as the 'Holy of Holies.' This event marks the beginning of the final phase of the seven years, specifically the last three and a half years, as Daniel notes, 'in the middle of the seven.'

Halfway through these seven years, or three and a half years (1,260 days), this man of evil will end sacrifices and offerings and establish an idol to be worshipped as a god. We know that God does not sanction this temple because Jesus has already established a New Covenant in His blood; therefore, they adhere to the Old Covenant Law of Moses.

We aim to pinpoint an instance when Israel can rebuild a temple without God's endorsement. This is a crucial element of the prophecy we are examining. However, let us pause and prepare for what is to come.

Footprints of Ezekiel

The Book of Ezekiel presents a mystery for our generation, especially since 1948, when Israel was restored to its land. Let us delve into this fascinating book, and then concentrate on the later chapters.

Ezekiel consists of three essential parts. The first three chapters document Ezekiel's call as a prophet. From there, until chapter 24, judgements are issued against Judah and Jerusalem. The final chapters, from 25 to the end, convey messages of hope and salvation.

Chapter 36, through to the end of Ezekiel, highlights the footprints. In this chapter, we witness Israel's restoration to the land. God expresses His anger towards the nations for their treatment of His people, and they return and flourish.

In the next chapter (37), God shows Ezekiel a 'Valley of Dry Bones.'

The hand of the LORD was on me, and he brought me out by the Spirit of the LORD and set me in the middle of a valley; it was full of bones. He led me back and forth among them, and I saw a great many bones on the floor of the valley, bones that were very dry. He asked me, 'Son of man, can these bones live?' I said, 'Sovereign LORD, you alone know' (Ezek. 37:1–3).

This puzzled me because God said He would restore His people, and then in the next chapter, He showed

Ezekiel dead people. After meditating, I concluded that the valley of dry bones referenced the future of His people. Furthermore, I came across images of Jews during the Holocaust depicting the bones of deceased and emaciated individuals, and it suddenly dawned on me that this prophecy referred to the Jews during World War Two. I had encountered this connection in some of my research but initially dismissed it. I recognised the connection with the following few verses.

Then he said to me, 'Prophesy to these bones and say to them, "Dry bones, hear the word of the LORD! This is what the Sovereign LORD says to these bones: I will make breath enter you, and you will come to life"' (Ezek. 37:4–5).

After the end of World War Two, what was dead came to life! Israel was reborn and became a nation once more in 1948. I was captivated by this. In Chapter 38, we see Israel back in the land. Following this, God becomes very angry with Israel; yet they eventually dwell in peace and safety. The flesh is back on the bones, but they remain spiritually dead.

In Chapters 38 and 39, war erupts. God declares that His name is being profaned (Ezekiel 38:7) and that He has turned away from them. In His wrath, God Himself summons warring nations against Israel. This event has not yet occurred. They are back in the land but do not enjoy peace or safety. They are spiritually dead yet thriving in perilous times. We will examine the details of these two chapters later, but when this war erupts, no one comes to Israel's aid!

Furthermore, after God saves Israel, he says:

'"I will no longer hide my face from them, for I will pour out my Spirit on the people of Israel", declares the Sovereign LORD' (Ezek. 39:29).

God will ultimately pour out His Spirit on Israel after this chapter. Even more remarkable is that in the subsequent chapters, 40–48, God seamlessly begins discussing the Millennial Period., including the newly constructed temple, and distributes the land among the twelve tribes of Israel.

Chapters 36–48 depict the prophetic signs between 1948 and Jesus' return. When God pours out His Spirit, they will recognise Him whom they have pierced, and all of Israel will be saved. Following this, we will enter the Millennial period with a temple blessed by God.

Now is the time to focus on the 'peace' described in Chapter 38 to understand Israel at peace, not sanctioned by God! He is angry with Israel and the world. Ezekiel 33–48 outlines a path that leads to restoration and the Millennium (1000 year reign). However, Chapter 38 indicates that Israel is initially at peace.

Chapters 38 and 39 detail the War of Gog and Magog, highlighting a conflict between Israel and a hostile force commanded by Gog, the leader of Magog. This battle occurs in the mountains of Israel, with the attackers advancing from the north and southwest. God intervenes, unleashing earthquakes, heavy rains, hail, fire and sulphur to destroy Gog and his invading forces, ultimately saving Israel. It is important to note that this differs from the Gog and Magog War mentioned in Revelation 20.

An extraordinary verse in Ezekiel 38:8:

After many days, you will be called to arms. In future years, you will invade a land that has recovered from war, whose people were gathered from many nations to the mountains of Israel, which had long been desolate. They had been brought out from the nations, and now all of them live in safety (Ezek. 38:8).

The Jews have returned from the nations to the land of Israel, which has long been desolate, and now they live seemingly safely. However, this peace is not what it seems. God will bring war to the land of Israel at a time when they are living in what appears to be peace and have recovered from conflict. It is evident that the Lord does not establish this period of peace:

You will say, 'I will invade a land of unwalled villages; I will attack a peaceful and unsuspecting people—all of them living without walls and without gates and bars.

I will plunder and loot and turn my hand against the resettled ruins and the people gathered from the nations, rich in livestock and goods, living at the centre of the land' (Ezek. 38:11–12).

Israel has never truly experienced the peace and safety mentioned in this verse since returning to the land. They have continually faced exile or assault from enemies. Living 'without gates and walls' symbolises their assurance of being free from attacks. Nevertheless, they are still destined to be assaulted!

God Himself places thoughts of war in the mind of Gog, the leader of a northern land. He assembles a coalition of nations to attack Israel, which lives in peace and security. The Jews have returned from the countries where they were exiled and now live safely. Why is God removing peace from Israel?

'"I will make known my holy name among my people Israel. I will no longer let my holy name be profaned, and the nations will know that I, the LORD, am the Holy One in Israel"' (Ezek. 39:7).

God describes His Holy name as 'profaned,' indicating that it has been disrespected by people on Earth. He also mentions 'hiding His face from them,' which signifies His rejection of the Israelites.

This peace has been established without God. I believe this is the same covenant (treaty of peace) mentioned in Daniel 9:27. This peace and security in Israel violate His name. However, God comes to Israel's aid because no one else will!

My question to the Lord was, 'Where is America in all of this?' Why isn't America supporting Israel? We know that America has shown strong support for Israel, particularly since President Trump assumed office and the attack on Iran! The passage indicates that God saves Israel. Then it suddenly struck me: the Church is no longer on Earth! Without the Church, antisemitism in the world would have intensified. Nations may protest, yet they fail to assist Israel. Ultimately, it is God who rescues them from this crisis.

Observe the devastation that God orchestrates, as described towards the end of chapter 39.

On that day I will give Gog a burial place in Israel, in the valley of those who travel east of the Sea. It will block the way of travelers, because Gog and all his hordes will be buried there. So it will be called the Valley of Hamon Gog. For seven months the Israelites will be burying them in order to cleanse the land (Ezek. 39:11–12).

God removed this peace because it was deceptive and anti-God; I believe it refers to the first seal our Lord opened in Revelation chapter 6. This first seal is a significant event that sets the stage for the unfolding of God's plan. Note the devastation in verse 12.

Let us establish the context for chapter 6 in the Book of Revelation. The previous chapter records God as holding a scroll bound by seven seals. The scroll details the judgements that must take place on Earth before the Lord Jesus can establish His kingdom and fulfil Daniel 9:24.

To reiterate:

- 'To finish transgression'
- 'To put an end to sin'
- 'To atone for wickedness'
- 'To bring in everlasting righteousness'
- 'To seal up vision and prophecy'
- 'To anoint the most holy'

In the previous chapter, Revelation 5, the Lamb of God is portrayed as the only one capable of taking the scroll, opening it and initiating the end times. During the tribulation, God declares war. Believers are removed, like Noah, and saved from the horror. After this point, the Church is not mentioned again until chapter 22 of Revelation. John, the author, sees this scroll—God's Battle Plan. It contains writing on both sides. We will now read the first four verses of Revelation 6 to determine when peace might be established between the nations and Israel, as described in Ezekiel 38 and Revelation 6:1–4.

I watched as the Lamb opened the first of the seven seals. Then I heard one of the four living creatures say in a voice like thunder, 'Come!' I looked, and there before me was a white horse! Its rider held a bow, and he was given a crown, and he rode out as a conqueror bent on conquest (Rev. 6:1–2).

Jesus opens the first of the seven seals, and in verse two, we see a rider on a white horse who is given a crown. The white horse is a symbol often associated with righteousness in biblical prophecy. This rider receives a crown, signifying his rulership. He is given a bow but no arrows, making him a conqueror without arms. It is important to clarify that the rider on a white horse in Revelation 6 is not Jesus; it represents deception. Let us compare this rider to Jesus on His white horse. This white horse symbolises trickery. It is not Jesus, as some suggest! Let us turn to Revelation 19 to see Jesus on His white horse for a clear contrast!

'I saw heaven standing open, and there before me was a white horse, whose rider is called Faithful and True. With justice, he judges and wages war' (Rev. 19:11).

This rider has a name and is a judge; He wages war.

'His eyes are like blazing fire, and on his head are many crowns. He has a name written on him that no one knows but He himself' (Rev. 19:12).

He has many crowns on His head, but He is not given them; they are His by right. He has a name.

'He is dressed in a robe dipped in blood, and his name is the Word of God' (Rev. 19:13).

We now know who He is. He is Jesus, the Word of God, who came in the flesh.

'The armies of heaven were following him, riding on white horses and dressed in fine linen, white and clean' (Rev. 19:14).

This army belongs to Jesus and comprises His bride, the Old Testament saints, and the tribulation martyrs. Angels are never depicted wearing 'fine white linen, clean and white.' The army that follows Jesus is described as pure, and only Jesus' blood can attain this level of purity.

'Coming out of his mouth is a sharp sword with which to strike down the nations. "He will rule them with an iron sceptre." He treads the winepress of the fury of the wrath of God Almighty' (Rev. 19:15).

He has a weapon called a sword—nothing like the rider of Revelation 6:2.

The rider of Revelation 6:2 will be a ruler on Earth, as he is granted a crown. He possesses power, though not the power of God. He establishes peace on Earth, but not through war, as he is given no arrows for his bow. He aims to conquer through deception, which is demonic. He is successful because Satan supports him, enabling him to perform many miracles. Furthermore, we observe that there is indeed peace on Earth. A lie is being sold to the world! They believe the lie because the Holy Spirit permits this delusion. Reading on.

*When the Lamb opened the second seal, I heard the second living creature say, 'Come!' Then another horse came out, a fiery red one. Its rider was given **power to take peace from the earth** and to make people kill each other. To him was given a large sword* (Rev. 6:3).

A fiery red horse signifies war and *takes peace from the earth*. This rider is granted the power to strip the established peace from the world, as it is not of God; therefore, this peace is demonic. Armed with a large sword, this rider destroys this peace.

In Daniel 9:27, Satan's messenger establishes peace on Earth by creating a covenant. This agent of Satan will establish a peace treaty with many individuals, including the Jewish residents of the land in the future, resulting in a misleading peace that God does not support.

He will confirm a covenant with many for one 'seven.' In the middle of the 'seven', he will put an end to sacrifice and offering. And at the temple, he will set up an abomination that causes desolation, until the end that is decreed is poured out on him (Dan. 9:27).

He establishes a covenant with multiple nations for seven years, allowing the Jews to rebuild their temple.

Halfway through, he enters the newly constructed temple and commits an act of desecration. At this point, I believe the second red fiery horse of Revelation is unleashed upon the earth, as we have seen. This rider holds the authority to take peace from the world. This occurs halfway through these seven years, and God begins to judge the earth because this man sets up an idol. Both Daniel and Jesus refer to this as an abomination.

What an intriguing puzzle, and more to come. Who is this man, and can we reveal more about him in this mystery? Paul refers to him as the man of lawlessness in 2 Thessalonians 2. Before delving deeper, let us make clear the context!

Paul aims to clarify misconceptions among the saints regarding the return of Jesus Christ and the Day of the Lord—two separate events. The saints faced intense persecution, leading them to believe they were already experiencing the initial phase of the Day of the Lord, particularly the Tribulation Period. Although John had not yet written the Book of Revelation, they understood the profound distress described by 'The Day of the Lord' (Zephaniah 1:14-16). Additionally, rumours suggested that the apostles believed and taught that this 'Day of the Lord' had already begun. He takes steps to correct them!

Concerning the coming of our Lord Jesus Christ and our being gathered to him, we ask you, brothers and sisters, not to become easily unsettled or alarmed by the teaching allegedly from us—whether by a prophecy or by word of mouth or by letter—asserting that the day of the Lord has already come. Don't let anyone deceive you in any way, for that day will not come until the rebellion occurs and the man of lawlessness is revealed, the man doomed to destruction. He will oppose and will exalt himself over everything that is called God or is worshipped, so that he sets himself up in God's temple, proclaiming himself to be God (2 Thess. 2:1–4).

The final verse alludes to the man described in previous scriptures and the reconstructed temple. This person asserts his divine status and demands worship as a god within the temple, a scenario not witnessed during Paul or John's era. As a result, God's name is being disrespected.

When will this be? Let us look more closely at verse three.

'Don't let anyone deceive you in any way, for that day will not come until the rebellion occurs and the man of lawlessness is revealed, the man doomed to destruction' (2 Thess. 2:3).

We must consider two significant events: the 'rebellion' and the 'man of lawlessness.'

Since the time of Adam and Eve, humanity has rebelled, yet this rebellion has a distinct character.

When an individual is unveiled and sets up an idol to be worshipped, it becomes the 'abomination' referred to by Jesus, which can be understood in the context of Daniel's final 'seven' years, as the 'man of lawlessness' establishes this idol. This rebellion concerns the apostasy during the Great Tribulation, a period when the world embraces Satan and accepts his mark. Until that time, he is being held back, and eventually, it is Satan himself who possesses this man and drives him on.

'For the secret power of lawlessness is already at work, but the one who now holds it back will continue to do so till he is taken out of the way' (2 Thess. 2:7).

However, the power of lawlessness is currently restrained.

Chapter Nine - The One Who Holds Back

Before proceeding, let us consider what holds back evil. The Lord Jesus instructs His disciples to wait for the Holy Spirit, their helper, whom He will send. After Jesus' ascension, the mission of the Holy Spirit was to establish His church and nurture His Bride. Jesus promises to remain with us and guide us into all truth.

The seventh verse's phrase 'the man of lawlessness' suggests it refers to a specific individual. Behind this person can be identified a malevolent force, Satan. Furthermore, the powers and principalities of the heavenly realms will also be involved.

We need to consider who possesses the authority to restrain the entire demonic realm, including Satan, as lawlessness originates from there. Has God granted this power to any angel or human? I firmly believe the answer is no. Only God the Holy Spirit can restrain the entire angelic realm and Satan. To control all these beings, one must be present everywhere simultaneously to understand the situation. No created being can achieve such omnipresence or indeed have the power. The presence of the Holy Spirit within every believer serves as a shield against evil, including the man of lawlessness, as He maintains the truth. Without the Holy Spirit, deception thrives.

'But the Advocate, the Holy Spirit, whom the Father will send in my name, will teach you all things and will remind you of everything I have said to you' (John 14:26).

The disciples knew the Holy Spirit and had experienced His work in their lives, witnessing Him working through the Lord Jesus. *'He dwells with you and will be in you.'* Before Pentecost, in the Old Testament, the Holy Spirit came upon specific individuals and dwelt with them, contingent upon their holy lives. However, since Pentecost, when a person believes in the Lord Jesus, the Holy Spirit permanently resides in that individual's life. The Holy Spirit is called the Spirit of Truth because His teachings exalt Christ as the truth. The world cannot accept the Holy Spirit because it does not recognise Him. Unbelievers often require evidence before embracing 'faith.' When the Holy Spirit ceases to constrain and withdraws, the truth fades, leading to profound delusion and lawlessness.

The Old Testament illustrates that an individual anointed by the Holy Spirit can forfeit that anointing, as highlighted in David's prayer in Psalm 51.

'Create in me a pure heart, O God, and renew a steadfast spirit within me. Do not cast me from your presence or take your Holy Spirit from me' (Ps. 51:10).

'Do not take your Holy Spirit from me.' David was well-acquainted with the Holy Spirit and feared losing Him as a companion. The Lord would never leave His bride unprotected. The Holy Spirit is never removed from a believer who has experienced true conversion, although He may be grieved by sinful behaviour. The Spirit came in Christ's name to represent His interests. He did not come to glorify Himself but to draw men and women to the Saviour. 'He will teach you all things,' said the Lord. He accomplished this through the apostles' spoken ministry and then through the written Word of God, which we have today. The Holy Spirit brings to remembrance all that the Saviour taught and records it in His Word. He speaks the truth. If He departs, so does the truth; what remains in its place is a lie, namely deception.

In the Old Testament, the Holy Spirit's role was to assist Israel in demonstrating God's righteousness through their deeds and the resulting blessings from obedience. Nevertheless, they frequently fell short and faced God's discipline. The Holy Spirit anointed select individuals, including prophets and judges, to reveal their shortcomings and encourage the Israelites to return to God. Thus, He contributed to restraining evil.

Today, the Holy Spirit's mission is to build the Church of God and proclaim that Jesus is the way, the truth and the life. He is her companion and will never leave her.

He restrains Satan's power and the demonic realm. He continuously dwells in the world through the Church, which has always been crucial in preventing society from succumbing to the overwhelming tide of lawlessness. At one point, Paul mentions that the Spirit will be 'taken out of the way' from His restraining work, allowing sin to dominate humanity. He does not abandon the world but permits evil to prevail. In the past, God, through His Spirit, initiated 'revivals' when darkness overwhelmed the Church.

He cannot forsake the Church on Earth; He remains its companion. This indicates His return to a prior role, where He anoints select individuals with truth and empowers them to prophesy, as illustrated in the Old Testament. This will be His function during the Great Tribulation, lasting seven years. While He will not restrain evil, His presence will still be felt; He cannot abandon the earth because He is omnipresent. However, His role has evolved. He persists in sharing the gospel by anointing individuals or groups. Since the Church is absent on Earth, it can no longer spread the message of Christ.

When the Holy Spirit removes the Church, acting as a stumbling block to Satan, a man granted a crown of rulership will be revealed. He Is the same man who will establish a covenant with 'the many' and the Jewish people, and his deceit will go unchallenged. This man is driven by Satan, whose purpose is to lead people into worshipping him. The truth disappears in the absence of God's Spirit.

The coming of the lawless one is according to the working of Satan, with all power, signs, and lying wonders, and with all unrighteous deception among those who perish, because they did not receive the love of the truth, that they might be saved. And for this reason God will send them strong delusion, that they should believe the lie, that they all may be condemned who did not believe the truth but had pleasure in unrighteousness (2 Thess. 2:9–12).

When will this lawless individual be exposed to the world? Right now, Satan has access to Heaven. Let us investigate this! In Revelation 12, we find that there is a conflict in Heaven.

Setting the context, a war breaks out in Heaven, with Michael and his angels on one side and the dragon (Satan) with his angels on the other. This occurs during the middle of the Tribulation. Michael, the archangel, is associated with Israel (Daniel 12:1). The archangel Michael is mentioned because God has designated him as Israel's guardian. He appears in a 'time of distress' that has not been seen since the dawn of nations.

Then war broke out in heaven. Michael and his angels fought against the dragon, and the dragon and his angels fought back. But he was not strong enough, and they lost their place in heaven. The great dragon was hurled down—that ancient serpent called the devil, or Satan, who leads the whole world astray. He was hurled to the earth and his angels with him (Rev. 12:7–9).

When Satan is cast out of Heaven, his mischief intensifies. He empowers a man known as the lawless one, and as the Holy Spirit no longer restrains evil, Satan implements his plan to establish himself as an object of worship in the rebuilt temple. Deception and miracles abound.

The Bible is indeed a jigsaw puzzle, but the breadcrumbs are present. Let us summarise what we have discussed: Daniel prays for the temple's restoration. His prayer is answered, but God reveals the future of his nation, Israel.

First, it will take forty-nine years, or 'one seven,' to rebuild the Second Temple. Then, from the time of the rebuilding of Jerusalem, another 434 years, or 'sixty-two sevens,' will pass for the Messiah (the Anointed One) to arrive among His people and be killed (cut off). It is fascinating to examine the date of Jesus' crucifixion, as there is compelling evidence that He died precisely as this prophecy indicates but we cannot tarry.

One 'seven,' or seven years, remains. During this final period, a man will make peace with Israel and allow them to rebuild a temple that God does not endorse. Halfway through, this man establishes an idol in the reconstructed temple for people to worship. Then, Jesus unleashes the world's judgement by opening the second seal in the scroll of Revelation 6, thereby ending this false peace.

The period between the 'sixty-two' sevens and the final 'seven' represents the time dedicated to the Church; it is the current era. That was a marathon, but there is more. To illustrate this, let us examine Daniel chapter 12, where I mentioned the archangel Michael as the one God appointed as Israel's guardian. Michael is the guardian spirit of the Jewish people; when trouble reaches its peak, whether national or international, help is close at hand.

Chapter Ten – Bittersweet Scroll

The last chapter of Daniel focuses on Israel, his nation. Gabriel delivers God's message concerning His people. The book's themes include prophecy grounded in Jewish history and the portrayal of the end times. Daniel chapter 12 examines the end times and the destiny of his people.

I have encountered individuals who attempt to spiritualise certain aspects of the Bible to align with their own beliefs. I have been corrected by those who assert that the Old Testament no longer applies because everything was fulfilled in Christ; therefore, they may not even read it, considering it irrelevant.

It is often stated that all prophecies in the New Testament relate to the Church, as God has turned away from the Jews. The Bible should be read literally, except when the context suggests a different approach. For example, the text may adopt a symbolic, figurative or literary style, requiring varied interpretation. In these instances, it is essential to compare scripture with scripture before deciding.

As previously noted, the Church Fathers continued what we now identify as antisemitism. They focused exclusively on matters concerning the Church. At that time and after the Diaspora, Israel did not exist as a nation, and its people were dispersed across the globe. However, they have returned; prophecies have come alive once more, and Israel's salvation is assured, as prophesied in the Old and New Testaments. Now, let us proceed!

We can connect Daniel to Revelation. A conversation occurs between two men dressed in linen (it does not specify 'fine white linen'). They are messengers of God, and Daniel overhears their discussion.

'One of them said to the man clothed in linen, who was above the waters of the river, "How long will it be before these astonishing things are fulfilled?"' (Dan. 12:6)

Daniel is listening and needs clarification. We are not reviewing the chapter verse by verse; I only want to focus on Chapter 12 and its connection to Revelation.

I heard, but I did not understand. So, I asked, 'My lord, what will the outcome of all this be?' He replied, 'Go your way, Daniel, because the words are rolled up and sealed until the time of the end' (Dan. 12:8).

The words are tightly rolled and sealed until the conclusion. This refers to the scroll John was instructed to consume in Revelation 10. Let us set the scene. This chapter shifts our attention from the judgements taking place on Earth. In Chapters 6 to 16 of Revelation, God's wrath is poured out in response to humanity's rebellion. Chapter 10 acts as an interlude, where a mighty angel presents a scroll to John.

Then the voice that I had heard from heaven spoke to me once more: 'Go, take the scroll that lies open in the hand of the angel who is standing on the sea and on the land.' So I went to the angel and asked him to give me the little scroll. He said to me, 'Take it and eat it. It will turn your stomach sour, but "in your mouth, it will be as sweet as honey."' I took the little scroll from the angel's hand and ate it. It tasted as sweet as honey in my mouth, but when I had eaten it, my stomach turned sour. Then I was told, 'You must prophesy again about many peoples, nations, languages and kings' (Rev. 10:8–11).

The sweetness of the message signifies the forgiveness it offers in John's mouth. In contrast, the bitterness in his gut arises from God's wrath, eventually bringing reconciliation for some. This bittersweet scroll is the one John is told to consume. It was written by Daniel but remained sealed until the end, as noted in Daniel 12:9. Its contents are now unveiled. Let us read from Daniel 12:10, where we see another connection to the messages of Jesus and John in Revelation.

'Many will be purified, made spotless and refined, but the wicked will continue to be wicked. None of the

wicked will understand, ***but those who are wise will understand'*** (Dan. 12:10).

Delusion will be prevalent during these seven years of turmoil. The next verse refers to an abomination Jesus mentioned and a specific count of days. Only a small group, those empowered by the Holy Spirit, can endure this time.

'From the time that the daily sacrifice is abolished and the abomination that causes desolation is set up, there will be 1,290 days. Blessed is the one who waits for and reaches the end of the 1,335 days' (Dan. 12:11–12).

The daily offerings will cease, and this idol will be placed within the temple for worship.

'And I will appoint my two witnesses, and they will prophesy for 1,260 days, clothed in sackcloth' (Rev. 11:3).

These two men proclaim the gospel; however, our focus is on the 1,290. This duration pertains to the latter segment of the Great Tribulation, lasting three and a half years, calculated according to the 360-day Hebrew lunar calendar. It is crucial to consider the context, culture and audience. The Holy Spirit empowers these witnesses.

The time frame mentioned here aligns with that outlined in Daniel 12. These two witnesses are often associated with the figures who spoke with Jesus during the Transfiguration or with Elijah and Elisha from the Old Testament. Furthermore, Zechariah 4 refers to two olive trees. These two witnesses pose significant challenges to Satan and the world. We will examine Revelation 11 for further details.

And I will appoint my two witnesses, and they will prophesy for 1,260 days, clothed in sackcloth. They are 'the two olive trees' and the two lampstands, and 'they stand before the Lord of the earth.' If anyone tries to harm them, fire comes from their mouths and devours their enemies. This is how anyone who wants to harm them must die (Rev. 11:3–5).

These two, chosen by the Holy Spirit, will confront evil throughout their mission. They will be in Jerusalem, massively challenging the forces of darkness and the earth's inhabitants. Empowered by the Holy Spirit, they will spread the gospel and defend against Satan's influence.

Ultimately, God permits their deaths, after which Daniel announces that the daily sacrifices will end. During the thirty days between 1,260 and 1,290, when these witnesses died, Satan abolished the daily sacrifice, resulting in the establishment of an idol in the temple for people to worship him. Individuals from every nation, tribe and tongue—in other words—the entire world looks upon these two witnesses for three and a half days, rejoicing in their demise. God is meticulous about time. They have been prophesying for 1,260 days, or three and a half years, as mentioned in verse three earlier in the passage.

The witnesses will be miraculously shielded from harm for three and a half years. Fire from their mouths devours their enemies, rendering it impossible to harm them. For 1,260 days, they preached the gospel and endeavoured to share the truth with the world, performing miracles along the way. However, when they are killed, their bodies lie unburied for three and a half days. Then, God raises them from the dead, and they ascend to Heaven. God's wrath descends upon the earth as the judgement continues, and afterwards, in chapter 12, the Word states that Satan is cast out of Heaven.

Chapter Eleven – Outline of Revelation

Reading Revelation can be challenging since it is not presented chronologically. It is filled with figurative language and visions, requiring knowledge of parts of the Old and New Testaments and unfulfilled prophecy. The book is divided into sections; below is a simple guide to assist those who have avoided this fascinating text. Christians should read this book.

Chapter one establishes Jesus' pedigree and His place as the centre of the Church. He is the First and the Last.

Chapters two and three record the state of the churches during John's time and provide a prophetic picture of the Church through the ages, culminating in the last two churches, Philadelphia and Laodicea.

In ***chapters four and five***, John ascends to Heaven, an event that occurs after the message to the churches has concluded. In these chapters, John observes key events, with Jesus, the Lamb, being the only one to open a scroll. Jesus, identified as the Lion of the tribe of Judah, receives the scroll from God's hand.

This scroll contains God's judgements against the earth in the form of seven Seals, seven Trumpets and seven Bowls of God's anger and wrath, which will be unleashed upon the people of Satan and the world.

Chapters six to sixteen record these judgements poured out on the earth, but with interludes that break off and take us elsewhere to provide more detail.

For instance, chapter 7 enumerates 144,000 people from the twelve tribes of Israel, all mentioned as outlined in the Old Testament. These individuals are sealed as they are God's own. Their role is to share the gospel message during this time of judgement, as the Church is no longer present on Earth, ensuring the gospel remains accessible. Empowered by the Holy Spirit, they are identified as God's servants, actively ministering in the Church's absence. Satan relentlessly pursues them!

Individuals who risk their lives to assist Jews during this era of 'great distress' face pursuit and death. These are the 'sheep' referred to by Jesus in Matthew 25:31–46.

This is Israel's time before God. His nation is serving Him. If, as some believe, the Church is present here, they are mistaken. Some interpret this allegorically, claiming it refers to the Church, but that is untrue. God specifically describes the twelve tribes of Israel that make up this group of people.

Chapter ten recounts the angel and the scroll mentioned earlier, which John is instructed to eat. We learn that it is both sweet and bitter, representing the offer of salvation or judgement.

Chapter eleven records the two witnesses who oppose Satan and call upon the world to hear Jesus' message.

Chapter fourteen describes the 144,000 (of chapter 7) in Heaven with God. Following this, the gospel message is entrusted to angels for dissemination. Notice that when the Church vanishes, Jesus is concerned that the message of salvation continues to be heard.

He first seals 144,000. Then, two witnesses appear to oppose Satan and keep the message of Salvation active. Once they are removed, because the situation worsens, angels take over this crucial task (Revelation 14:6).

Chapters seventeen and eighteen record the fall of Babylon.

Chapters 19–22 describe Satan's imprisonment, Jesus' 1000-year reign on Earth, a great battle, and the creation of the New Heaven and New Earth. The word millennium comes from the Latin word 'mille,' meaning a thousand.

Let us move on.

Chapter Twelve - The Millennium

The gospel message is so vital that God seals people to fulfil this task through His Holy Spirit during the Great Tribulation, a time of immense difficulty. When Satan is cast out of Heaven, angels proclaim the gospel (Revelation 12:7). The earth is a battleground; Satan has been expelled from Heaven and is raging across the world. Nevertheless, Christ must still be offered to everyone. It cannot be claimed, 'I did not know.'

What happens next? After Satan is defeated and cast out of Heaven, he realises his time is limited. Following the defeat of the world and the Lamb's wedding supper mentioned in Revelation 19, Satan is bound for one thousand years, as outlined in the first part of Revelation 20.

And I saw an angel coming down out of heaven, having the key to the Abyss and holding in his hand a great chain. He seized the dragon, that ancient serpent, who is the devil, or Satan, and bound him for a thousand years. He threw him into the Abyss, and locked and sealed it over him, to keep him from deceiving the nations anymore until the thousand years were ended.

After that, he must be set free for a short time (Rev. 20:1–3).

Satan is imprisoned for a thousand years, during which neither he nor his demons can deceive the nations until he is released once more. I asked my companion about the purpose of this situation.

The millennial kingdom will be Jesus' future reign on Earth, specifically in Jerusalem. God will redeem and make everyone who enters that kingdom righteous. Those redeemed will be divided into two groups: those with glorified physical bodies and those with natural, earthly bodies. The latter group consists of those who emerged from the Great Tribulation period, never worshipped the beast, and are born again. To understand this, we must first review the creation pattern described in Genesis 1, which we also call God's plan of redemption.

Jesus entered the world as the 'light of the world.' On the first day of creation, He was the light that held power over darkness. On the fourth day, the world was illuminated by the stars in the heavens. Jesus took on flesh and dwelt among us, becoming the world's light. He taught us about the Father in Heaven.

My companion then encouraged me to examine the first Passover Lamb, which was kept for four days as the sacrifice intended to protect the Israelites from the tenth plague inflicted upon the Egyptians.

We connected Jesus' final days, reflecting the first Passover Lamb, to the initial four days of creation.

Jesus entered His house in Jerusalem and received a warm welcome. He was praised as He rode through the city gates. The timing of Jesus' crucifixion is symbolic of the First Passover. Just as the Passover lambs were sacrificed to commemorate the Israelites' deliverance from Egypt, Jesus was sacrificed for humanity's salvation from sin.

Four days later, He was crucified. Three days after, He rose from the dead, defeating death and the spiritual forces in the heavens while gaining control of 'Death and Hades.' The last three days represented a spiritual victory. Now, He must assume physical control of the earth to liberate creation from the curse of sin and decay. A physical return to the world to rule and reign from Jerusalem will bring peace to creation. This is the seventh day of rest, as described in the creation narrative. God fulfils all His promises during this period of peace on Earth. Let us clarify the purpose of these thousand years. Satan and his forces have been vanquished and imprisoned. So why hasn't God entered eternity? Everything is fulfilled, or is it?

Satan's emissaries have been cast into the lake of fire, from which there is no return, while Satan himself is merely chained and confined in an abyss. This situation arises because those in the lake of fire cannot return;

there is no chance of escape. However, God has other plans for Satan!

And I saw an angel coming down out of heaven, having the key to the Abyss and holding in his hand a great chain. He seized the dragon, that ancient serpent, who is the devil, or Satan, and bound him for a thousand years (Rev. 20:1–2).

He is then let loose again! Why?

'He threw him into the Abyss, and locked and sealed it over him, to keep him from deceiving the nations anymore until the thousand years were ended. After that, he must be set free for a short time' (Rev. 20:3).

When set free, he incites the world against the Lord, who is ruling and reigning from Jerusalem.

When the thousand years are over, Satan will be released from his prison and will go out to deceive the nations in the four corners of the earth—Gog and Magog—and to gather them for battle. In number, they are like the sand on the seashore (Rev. 20:7–8).

The nations of the world have experienced peace and safety for 1,000 years. However, when Satan is released, the people of the world come together to wage war against Jesus and His followers.

They marched across the breadth of the earth and surrounded the camp of God's people, the city he loves.

But fire came down from heaven and devoured them. And the devil, who deceived them, was thrown into the lake of burning sulfur, where the beast and the false prophet had been thrown. They will be tormented day and night forever and ever (Rev. 20:9–10).

To understand why we need to revisit the end of the tribulation period, consider those who endured the Great Tribulation and entered Jesus' 1000-year reign on Earth.

Although these individuals were saved from great distress and were born again, they still possessed sinful natures and entered the millennium in their natural bodies. They would teach their children about Jesus and what He did for them, but those children would also inherit this sinful nature. These children still face the same choice: to choose Jesus or not! He now rules and reigns from Jerusalem *for all to see*.

Unlike us, they do not enter this peaceful time on Earth in resurrection bodies. The devastation during the Great Tribulation will lessen the number of people entering this period, known as the Millennium. Many have tried to calculate what this may imply, but if you read about the horrors of God's judgement in chapters 6–16, you can envision the bodies of the dead piling up in the world. Ezekiel 39:11–12 offers us a clue:

On that day I will give Gog a burial place in Israel, in the valley of those who travel east of the Sea. It will block the way of travelers, because Gog and all his hordes will be buried there. So it will be called the Valley of Hamon Gog. For seven months the Israelites will be burying them in order to cleanse the land (Ezek. 39:11–12).

For seven months, they have been burying the dead! This is just in Israel; think about the situation worldwide! Suddenly, there are fewer people left. Space is no longer an issue, and everyone has their own homes. Jesus will reign from Jerusalem, but conflicts still arise. Micah 4 provides a prophetic insight into this millennial era.

He will judge between many peoples and will settle disputes for strong nations far and wide. They will beat their swords into plowshares and their spears into pruning hooks. Nation will not take up sword against nation, nor will they train for war anymore. Everyone will sit under their own vine and under their own fig tree, and no one will make them afraid, for the LORD Almighty has spoken (Mic. 4:3–4).

Jesus must resolve disputes, and we are informed that all weapons will be abolished, leading to the end of war. There are about eight billion people on Earth and considering the number who will perish during the Great Tribulation, those who enter this Millennial period will likely number in the low billions. The global population is expected to grow during this time. God's promises to Israel will be fulfilled during Jesus'

1,000-year reign. First, He will fulfil His covenant with Abraham regarding the land. He also promised that Jesus would rule and reign on David's throne. All of God's promises are now realised in this unique time.

Of the greatness of his government and peace, there will be no end. He will reign on David's throne and over his kingdom, establishing and upholding it with justice and righteousness from that time on and forever. The zeal of the LORD Almighty will accomplish this (Isa. 9:7).

In one of Daniel's visions, he is shown a future time when Jesus will rule over the world.

He was given authority, glory and sovereign power; all nations and peoples of every language worshipped him. His dominion is an everlasting dominion that will not pass away, and his kingdom is one that will never be destroyed (Dan. 7:14).

We have a glimpse into the state of other life on Earth:

That the creation itself will be liberated from its bondage to decay and brought into the freedom and glory of the children of God. We know that the whole creation has been groaning as in the pains of childbirth right up to the present time (Rom. 8:21–22).

Read and ponder Isaiah 11, where we find animals lose their fear of man and each other in Jesus' reign.

He will wear righteousness like a belt and truth like an undergarment. In that day the wolf and the lamb will live together; the leopard will lie down with the baby goat. The calf and the yearling will be safe with the lion, and a little child will lead them all. The cow will graze near the bear. The cub and the calf will lie down together. The lion will eat hay like a cow (Isa. 11:5–7).

Many verses relate to the state of this peaceful period. However, we find that not all humanity is willing.

'To all who are victorious, who obey me to the very end. To them I will give authority over all the nations. They will rule the nations with an iron rod and smash them like clay pots' (Rev. 2:26–27).

Life on Earth is perfect. Everyone has a place to live, and there is no illness, mental health concerns or crime; the Lord resolves all issues immediately. In contrast to Earth's residents, the world's leaders will be regenerate, Spirit-filled saints in resurrected bodies. Consequently, during this period, we, the members of the Church, will serve as ambassadors, administering Jesus' judgements to the nations of Earth.

Never again will there be in it an infant who lives but a few days, or an old man who does not live out his years; the one who dies at a hundred will be thought a mere child; the one who fails to reach a hundred will be considered accursed. They will build houses and dwell in them, plant vineyards, and eat their fruit (Isa. 65:20–21).

No babies will die or be born prematurely. They will be delivered genetically pure. However, they will still possess a sinful nature. People will live significantly longer lives, but we will still observe instances of death. According to the Lord, individuals who do not reach the age of 100 will be considered cursed, suggesting that some are defiant. We can see humanity's sinful nature in action. Mankind does not require Satan or demons to demonstrate its inherent wickedness. The sinful nature remains present!

Children born during this time will not share the same experiences as the tribulation saints. They will, however, be taught about this dreadful period. The world's population is expected to surge, and they will enter an age of abundance, free from illness, disease and suffering. To coin a phrase, they are born with 'silver spoons' in their mouth.

This presents challenges for a world filled with individuals who still have a sinful nature. Nowadays, we tend to believe that if everything were perfect, life would be significantly better for people across the globe. No sickness, suffering or homelessness would exist, and everyone would coexist harmoniously. If we distributed wealth more evenly worldwide and ensured that everyone was well-fed, we would become better individuals. After all, we are good people, aren't we? This shows that even though people can see Jesus and witness the presence of God on Earth, it is still not enough.

This millennial period is one of the reasons God set aside to demonstrate that, regardless of their circumstances, fallen people are never satisfied. They seek peace and harmony apart from God. They do not wish to honour God for what He has given them. They desire to act as they please, but the life within them belongs to God! With Satan locked away, we cannot blame him or the demons.

The period of abundance raises questions for many who cannot accept that God chooses some and not others. Our family, friends and loved ones are dear to us, and we pray that they may be with us in Heaven. Why does God choose? Why does God not select everyone? The truth is that if God did not choose, none of us would be in Heaven. During this time of peace and abundance, we find treachery when God shows His love and Jesus is offered to all. When Satan is released, many join him in rebellion, like grains of sand on the seashore. At the end of this 1000-year reign of Jesus on Earth, many align with Satan. Jesus is present, and everyone is aware of Him, but Satan can amass a colossal force against Him and His followers. Mankind sees Jesus but does not want to know.

When the thousand years are over, Satan will be released from his prison and will go out to deceive the nations in the four corners of the earth—Gog and Magog—and to gather them for battle. In number, they are like the sand on the seashore (Rev. 20:7–8).

This will be the final War of Wars before we see a New Heaven and a New Earth: the Gog and Magog war. Billions will join Satan in rebellion against Jesus, illustrating the wickedness that still exists in humanity during this time. God demonstrates that without Him, and without being born again with a new nature, we are unfit to inhabit the 'New Heaven and the New Earth' that He will create. This old heaven and earth will dissolve once God puts down this immense rebellion.

God gives us life; His life dwells within us. He alone provides everything we ask for or desire. Without Him, we become mere shadows of what we are meant to be. Thus, even without demonic influence, we are still inclined towards evil.

After the Millennium, we encounter the hidden day: the New Heaven and the New Earth—the eighth day of creation that appears instantly. New beginnings! Everything is concealed in Christ. Jesus is the hidden day; He represents the eighth day of creation. His name in Hebrew provides a clue. The Hebrew alphabet assigns a number to each letter, and the numerical value of His name is 888, signifying 'new beginnings.' This is a reference to the Trinity and a new day. We have a clue to this at the end of Matthew 28:1, Mark 16:2 and John 20:1.

'After the Sabbath, at dawn on the first day of the week, Mary Magdalene and the other Mary went to look at the tomb' (Matt. 28:1).

'Very early on the first day of the week, just after sunrise, they were on their way to the tomb' (Mark 16:2).

'Early on the first day of the week, while it was still dark, Mary Magdalene went to the tomb and saw that the stone had been removed from the entrance' (John 20:1).

All three Gospels mention 'the first day of the week.' This marks a new beginning. It is the first day, yet it is also the eighth day. Mary Magdalene and the other Mary went to the tomb but found the stone rolled away. They conversed with angels who told them He had risen. This first day of the week is the eighth hidden day of creation. It represents a 'new beginning.' Now, all creation has a chance to be free from the curse of sin.

Importance of Christ

The Son is the image of the invisible God, the firstborn over all creation. For in him all things were created: things in heaven and on earth, visible and invisible, whether thrones or powers or rulers or authorities; all things have been created through him and for him. He is before all things, and in him all things hold together.

And he is the head of the body, the church; he is the beginning and the firstborn from among the dead, so that in everything he might have the supremacy (Col. 1:15–18).

Jesus represents the First Fruit, the Firstborn of both the New Heaven and the New Earth. Eternity commences with Him, marking the eighth day that continues endlessly.

Chapter Thirteen – Animal Sacrifice During the Millennium

My dissatisfaction grew as I listened to several knowledgeable pastors discuss this topic. A question was posed, 'Why will animal sacrifice be required during the millennium if Jesus has already died and shed his blood once and for all people?' This is a legitimate question.

Isaiah 56 and Jeremiah 33 reference burnt offerings and sacrifices in this time, indicating that all nations in the Millennium will gather in Jerusalem to observe the 'Feast of Tabernacles.' These nations will worship Jesus, who will reside among us during this period, or 'tabernacle' with us (live). But what is the purpose of animal sacrifice?

'Then the survivors from all the nations that have attacked Jerusalem will go up year after year to worship the King, the LORD Almighty, and to celebrate the Festival of Tabernacles' (Zech. 14:16).

Zechariah prophesied to the people of Judah after their 70-year exile in Babylon. Zechariah 42–46 reveals that during the Millennium, the Levitical system of sacrifices and offerings—including the burnt offering, the oblation, the peace offering, the sin and trespass offerings, and the drink offering—will be reinstated.

So, why must these animals be sacrificed if Jesus has paid for the world's sins? We have established that people will still be sinful. They live in peace and safety and will not experience death to the same extent that we do in this age. The animals are peaceful and unafraid of humans, and it seems humans will adopt a vegetarian diet. Thus, the shedding of blood will be quite strange and yet, the nations of the world will have to go up to Jerusalem to witness innocent animals being killed.

They will already know about Jesus' death and resurrection. As ambassadors of Christ, we will be rulers and teachers, spreading the gospel message of salvation. However, death will be unfamiliar to them, so the shedding of blood will be a considerable shock.

The killing of animals for their blood demonstrates the necessity of blood for the forgiveness of sins. Nevertheless, going to Jerusalem illustrates that innocent animal blood is not sufficient, as it must occur year after year. However, what Jesus did was far more significant; His blood atoned for all sins, for all time. Those who accept Him as Lord and Saviour will be forgiven and become part of His family. Animal sacrifice during the millennium conveys the gospel message that without the shedding of innocent blood, sin cannot be forgiven. The cost of sin must be shown to these people born in peace and safety! You must be born again.

Chapter Fourteen - Why Be Born Again?

We have traced all seven days of the creation narrative and see that God provided Moses with His outline of redemption in this account. On the very last day, we observe from God's Word that He grants the earth 1,000 years of peace with Jesus ruling and reigning from Jerusalem. We also find that humans still possess a sinful nature, as most of humanity consists of individuals primarily driven by transactional motives. This illustrates the impact of sin on us.

During this period, God fulfils every promise made to Israel, His chosen nation. The world observes the fulfilment of Abraham's covenant concerning the land and witness Jesus reigning from Jerusalem. As a church composed of born-again, Spirit-filled believers, we actively participate in Christ's reign. Nevertheless, it is apparent that ultimately, billions will gather against our Lord and His followers, with Satan mustering an army to oppose God's faithful on Earth. This situation underscores the nature of unrepentant humanity.

After Satan's defeat comes the judgement, as detailed towards the end of Revelation Chapter 20. So, why be born again? There are two groups of created beings: angels and humans. Animals are also part of creation, but their purpose differs. A person who loved her pets asked me if they would be with her in Heaven. My companion prompted me to ask her if she believed that God loved her. The reply was positive, and then I asked if she believed God loved her pets. The answer was yes. I left it to her to understand that God loves all He has created.

Scripture reveals four distinct groups of individuals (male and female).

- Sons of God
- Sons of Abraham
- Sons of Adam
- Sons of Adoption

Sons of God

The clearest insight into these individuals comes from the Book of Job, one of the oldest texts in the Bible. This book tells the story of a man Satan was permitted to afflict. Though he had seven sons and considerable wealth, he ultimately faced a severe downfall, losing his riches and suffering from illness. Nevertheless, the compelling narrative begins in the first chapter of Job.

'One day, the angels came to present themselves before the LORD, and Satan also came with them (Job 1:6).

It presents a fascinating discourse between God and Satan; however, we will focus on verse 6. The *NIV* refers to angels, while the *NKJV* uses the term 'sons of God'.

'Now there was a day when the sons of God came to present themselves before the LORD, and Satan also came among them' (Job 1:6, *NKJV*)

'Sons of God' refers to angels, the first group of living beings created by God. They were made by His hand, not through sexual reproduction. Having lived in heaven in the presence of God some chose to follow Satan.

Sons of Abraham

Abraham served as the instrument of God's blessing for the world. The nation of Israel emerged from him due to a promise made to a childless couple; Isaac embodied that promise. Although some argue that Ishmael, being Abraham's firstborn, was meant to receive the blessing, he was born of the flesh rather than the promise. Christ would not come through Ishmael but through Isaac. The individuals who pursued this promise, many of whom are mentioned in Hebrews 11, were kept in paradise until Jesus was offered as the first fruits. He saved them from within the Earth and took them to Heaven during that period. Essentially, these are the saints of the Old Testament. Now, let us look at Hebrews 11, commonly known as the 'Hall of Faith.'

'These all died in faith, not having received the promises, but having seen them afar off were assured of them, embraced them, and confessed that they were strangers and pilgrims on the earth' (Heb. 11:13, *NKJV*).

These are the 'Sons of Abraham'—sons of faith who looked forward to the promise—the Old Testament Saints.

Sons of Adam

Adam and Eve were created by the very hand of God, just like the angels. They were one flesh with Eve taken from Adam's side. They enjoyed a personal relationship with God until they chose disobedience. Consequently, God condemned them to both physical and spiritual death. Unfortunately, everyone born of Adam and Eve faces a curse and is destined for the 'lake of fire' alongside fallen angels.

Sin originates from Adam and is transmitted solely through the male lineage. God held Adam accountable, not Eve. This is illustrated in 1 Timothy 2:14. To provide context, Paul addresses Timothy, the son of a Greek father and a Jewish mother. Both his mother and grandmother were believers who taught him the Hebrew Bible from an early age. In this passage, he is urged to pray, but later in *verse 14*, Paul asserts the following:

'And Adam was not the one deceived; it was the woman who was deceived and became a sinner' (1 Tim. 2:14).

The inference here is that Adam's actions were a clear choice to disobey God. He was not being 'egged on' by Satan.

'Therefore, just as sin entered the world through one man, and death through sin, and in this way, death came to all people because all sinned' (Rom. 5:12).

Again, when Paul talks about resurrection in 1 Corinthians 5:22— 'as in Adam all die, so in Christ all will be made alive'— he is noting that the seed of man condemns us all. Although Eve was deceived, through her will come the Saviour. The seed of sin cannot contaminate Him because He is not born of man. By the power of the Holy Spirit, he can be fully human through Eve. That is why we must die and be separated from this physical body! We need to be delivered from the Adamic Body of Death into the Glorious Body of Christ; in brief, we need to be born again.

I hear the question: Why am I held responsible for Adam's sin? In contrast, God, without fault, chose to sacrifice Himself for all of us. He could have erased mankind and started anew. However, if you know the Bible, you understand that God does not retract His gifts. His unconditional love for us remains, yet He desires our love to be given freely! Every individual wants to live their life as they wish. It is my life and my body belongs to me! Nevertheless, we are granted life; God's life sustains us, and without His nurturing, we become unwell. The desires of the flesh, the desires of the eyes and the pride of life (1 John 2:16) lead us astray. In essence, the self within us places itself first.

The Millennium serves as a compelling example. God dwells with us on Earth, ruling and reigning from Jerusalem. Peace prevails and people receive everything they desire. There is no sickness, no war and homelessness has been eradicated. The land is bountiful and produces with little effort. However, at the end of this period with Jesus, the world unites with Satan to wage battle against Him. Humanity seeks control but is deceived as Satan desires to dominate them and craves worship as a god.

Sons of Adoption

When we die and are born again, the Father adopts us. Let Scripture speak for itself.

'He predestined us for adoption to sonship through Jesus Christ, in accordance with his pleasure and will' (Eph. 1:5).

'But when the set time had fully come, God sent his Son, born of a woman, born under the law, to redeem those under the law, that we might receive adoption to sonship' (Gal. 4:4–5).

When you die, you die to the law of sin and death. When you are born again, you transition from the line of Adam to an adopted child. Death is the great dividing line; it is either death to death or death to life!

Because you are his sons, God sent the Spirit of his Son into our hearts, the Spirit who calls out, 'Abba, Father.' So you are no longer a slave, but God's child; and since you are his child, God has made you also an heir (Gal. 4:6–7).

Nicodemus was puzzled by being born again; read the account when Jesus says, *'Very truly I tell you, no one can see the kingdom of God unless they are born again'* (John 3:3).

No one born of Adam can be with the Father.

Chapter Fifteen - How Can I Be Sure?

Life can present various challenges like a rollercoaster; however, this analogy may not fully capture the experience. Before discovering my spiritual path with the Lord, I primarily focused on my aspirations and goals. My ambitions revolved around seeking attention and the relationships I formed were often somewhat superficial. While your experiences may differ, we undeniably share commonalities during the moments that truly matter. In short, my neighbour was of little concern to me. Things did not change overnight when Jesus introduced Himself; it took years. I remained fleshly, still lustful, and prone to presenting myself to others as if I had everything sorted out.

Two things stood out during my early years with Christ. First, I became more aware of my language when speaking to others and swearing in my conversations began to feel distasteful. It took some time, but I eventually started to use language differently. Second, I began reading the Bible. Before that, it resembled a reference book on a shelf. No pictures and loads of words that I generally did not understand, much like one of those reference books on the top shelf of an extensive library, which seemed untouched and dusty. For those who remember old telephone directories, it felt like that for me!

After reading the New Testament and the Gospels several times, I reflected on the life of the man called Christ in detail. The Book of Revelation remained a mystery, and I did not always enjoy the Old Testament. Understanding the New Testament without knowledge of this part was particularly challenging, especially regarding prophecy.

The Bible teaches that God is not primarily concerned with people's outward appearances but focuses on the inner self, which we cannot hide. It guides us on what we should and should not do; however, breaking each of the Ten Commandments is still possible. Wow, that is quite a sweeping statement! While a person's actions may not violate God's laws, their desires, thoughts and words can.

For example, feelings of hate or lust may arise within an individual without necessarily leading to actions or, we can observe the opposite sex, and even if no actions take place, we can still commit adultery before God. I overheard a conversation between a couple. One stared at a person walking by for an unusually long time. The other remarked, 'I am here.' The response was, 'It's just eye candy.'

When you are alone with God, you can be sure you are born again when things like this begin to concern you about yourself. It is not merely 'window shopping.' The Holy Spirit will work in us to help us transition into the 'new man'. As a family, we have moved house many times. When I was in the forces, this was an integral part of our lives, and my family and I frequently moved from Scotland to Portsmouth. We eventually bought a house and settled down. Although I still had to travel, the family no longer faced upheaval. Years later, we purchased another home, and the items we accumulated while living in the first house were astonishing. There were things in the loft, in the outbuildings—everywhere! I never want to move from one house to another again! Clearing out, packing and cleaning before handing it over to the new owners took significant time and effort. The Holy Spirit helps us transition into the 'new man', but it requires time and effort.

After being a Christian for over forty years, I continue to move from the old self to the new. This is a lifelong journey. Through my companion's guidance, God's living and active Word has transformed me. If you cherish God's Word, you can be confident that His Spirit dwells within you and that you are reborn. The Bible is crucial for all Christians. I understand that some individuals may find it challenging to read. Fortunately, the Bible is now offered in various formats to improve accessibility.

Without genuine inner conversion, we cannot claim to belong to Christ. The Holy Spirit awaits at the door of our hearts, and when we invite Him in, that transformation will occur. Change is essential. A thought to add to this! If studying His word all your life does not transform your heart, watch out. To some, it is just ancient text that can be fascinating. To others, they concentrate on flaws that apparently question its worth. To many, it is just comforting. Change must happen by the inspiration of His Spirit and this only comes alive through reading His Word. The Spirit and the Word!

Over the years of my journey with Christ, I have taken actions and harboured thoughts that I truly regret. However, I have come to understand my frailties, and this understanding has slowly nurtured a deeper compassion for my neighbour. Acknowledging my shortcomings has opened my eyes to the necessity of forgiveness. Though challenging, negativity fades when I reflect on my vulnerabilities. This realisation aligns with the teaching to 'love your neighbour as you love yourself.'

In our journey with Christ, embracing self-love is crucial, but we should not let our flaws weigh us down. By treating ourselves with kindness and care, we naturally become more inclined to spread that kindness to others. Over time, genuine concern for our inner life before God flourishes. Neglecting this concern could lead us to question our dedication to Christ.

Exercise caution. The matters at hand extend beyond mere charitable giving in its various forms. Certain non-Christians may exemplify a level of character that surpasses that of Christians. The focus is on the disposition of the heart toward one's neighbour—extending forgiveness where appropriate and refraining from reactive behaviours in response to hurt. This lifelong journey is intricately connected to the myriad of emotional crossroads we encounter. However, it is essential to recognise that absolute perfection is not a prerequisite. Present your shortcomings to Christ and proceed accordingly. As we navigate through life, we continue to improve.

Final Summary

The millennium period clarifies why God chooses some and not others. We cannot see into the hearts of others, but God can. I would love for all my family and friends to go to Heaven, but they seek proof before committing. The millennium reign will provide all the evidence needed; yet in the end, countless will gather against our Lord like sand on the seashore. Living in a physically perfect world without want, with Jesus ruling and reigning in Jerusalem, is not for them.

Their downfall will arise from the lust of the flesh, the lust of the eyes and the pride of life. Concentrate on how God perceives us, not on what we attempt to present to Him and others!

Efforts to undermine prophecy have failed. Israel is now back in the land, and we are told that when we see these signs, *'He is at the door.'* Israel may experience an unsanctioned peace, but it will pay dearly when God permits a devastating attack from which only He can save them.

When the Holy Spirit withdraws, the Truth departs from the earth, resulting in widespread delusion during the Great Tribulation, as described in the Book of Revelation. However, Jesus comes with His army and restores order. Once the Millennium ends, we transition into a 'New Heaven and a New Earth'. Thanks be to God the Father of our Lord Jesus Christ.

Lastly, let us remember that the Pharisees often emphasised outward appearances, which Jesus spoke against. He truly cares about how we treat one another and warmly encourages us to share His love with our neighbours.

This account reflects nearly twenty years of experience in learning and teaching, during which I unknowingly prepared this work for God. As for the sermons presented, I have sincerely tried to document my sources for proper acknowledgement; regrettably, some have been lost to time or I could not remember them. Nevertheless, all inspiration is derived from our God.

Consequences mount daily in a world that denies the existence of God.

Amen.

Bibliography

[1] New International Version. Biblica, 2011 *(9930 words of 57216 without Bibliography or Foreword or back cover text) = 17.5%, totalling 374 verses)*

[2] The Holy Bible: New King James Version. (1982). Thomas Nelson. (10 verses)

[3] Young's Literal Translation - Published 1863, 1887, 1897

[4] Indentured Labour - © August 2017 Charles Rivers (digital page 28)

[5] Roger Price 'His Story' Rogerprice.co.uk

[6] Hammond, Dr. Peter, The Greatest Century of Missions (Christian Liberty Books, 2022)

[7] Dr Peter Hammond (Chapter 14, page 145) Kindle Edition 2022

[8] When a Nation Prays - Pastor Peter Simpson, Crown University Press 2022 Chapter 10 Page 95 (digital)

[9] Associates for Biblical Research 'The Origins of The Septuagint' biblearcheology.org

[10] Jews for Jesus; Jesus' last week March 9 2011

[11] Jay McCarl – Galilean Wedding (jaymccarl.com)

[12] Syriac versions of the Bible, December 17 2024, wikipedia.org/wiki/Syriac versions of the Bible

[13] wikiversity.org/wiki/Council of Nicaea (325A.D.) Public Domain

www.ingramcontent.com/pod-product-compliance
Lightning Source LLC
Chambersburg PA
CBHW030914090426
42737CB00007B/187

* 9 7 8 1 8 3 6 1 5 3 9 3 1 *